WEDDED BLISS

The Marriage of Art and Ceremony

PEABODY

ESSEX

MUSEUM

Salem, Massachusetts

Distributed by
University Press of
New England

Hanover and London

Published by the Peabody Essex Museum, Salem, Massachusetts, in conjunction with the exhibition *Wedded Bliss: The Marriage of Art and Ceremony*, April 26, 2008–September 14, 2008.

Distributed by University Press of New England
One Court Street,
Lebanon, NH 03766
www.upne.com

Printed in Italy
5 4 3 2 1

Peabody Essex Museum
East India Square
Salem, Massachusetts 01970
www.pem.org

Library of Congress Control Number: 2008922627
ISBN (cloth): 0-87577-214-5
ISBN (paper): 0-87577-215-3

Front cover: Advertising Art Photograph for Priscilla of Boston, ca. 1970 / Boston, Massachusetts / Gelatin silver print / Peabody Essex Museum

Back cover: Amrit and Rabindra Singh
Nyrmla's Wedding II, 1985–1986 / England / Poster paint, gouache, and gold dust on mountboard / Courtesy of the artists

Page 1: PLATE 1, Laura Coombs Hills (1859–1952)
The Bride, 1908 / Newburyport, Massachusetts / Watercolor on ivory / Museum of Fine Arts, Boston

Pages 2–3: PLATE 2, Sandy Skoglund (b. 1946)
The Wedding, 1994 / United States / Silver dye bleach (Cibachrome) / Columbus Museum of Art, Ohio / © 1994 Sandy Skoglund

Page 5: PLATE 3, Alex Katz (b. 1927)
Wedding Dress, 1993 / United States / Aquatint and etching / Courtesy of Barbara Krakow Gallery

Image credits begin on page 188.

Produced by Vern Associates, Inc., Newburyport, Massachusetts
www.vernassoc.com
Designed by Peter M. Blaiwas
Edited by Brian D. Hotchkiss
Printed and bound by Mondadori Printing, Verona, Italy

CONTENTS

PLATE 4

Wedding Dress, 1801
Salem, Massachusetts, made of fabric
imported from India / Cotton / Peabody
Essex Museum

Moon Shawl, ca. 1801 / Kashmir / Goats'
fleece / Peabody Essex Museum

In November 1801, the parlor of the Peirce
family home in Salem, Massachusetts,
was the setting for the wedding of Sally
Peirce, a merchant's daughter, and George
Nichols, a young sea captain who had just
returned from India. The bride's parents
commissioned architect and wood carver
Samuel McIntire to redecorate the east
parlor in preparation for the wedding.
Neoclassicism, an aesthetic style that
drew inspiration from art and architecture
of ancient Greece and Rome, influenced
both interior decoration and fashionable
dress of the day. Sally Peirce wore a bridal
ensemble that included a white muslin
dress, an imported shawl, and a lace
veil "put on turban fashion." The groom
purchased the sheer white striped cotton
fabric in Bombay, India, from the merchant
Nusserwanjee Maneckjee Wadia, for five
dollars per yard. The Indian merchant gave
Nichols a Kashmir moon shawl to take
back to his bride as a wedding present.
Made from the fleece of Kashmir goats,
these shawls were prized luxury textiles
in the international maritime trade. Even
at this early period in the nation's history,
international art and design influenced
American fashion and wedding attire. This
historic house is now owned by the Peabody
Essex Museum; the parlor was restored to
its original appearance in 2007.*

*Martha Nichols, ed., *George Nichols,
Salem Shipmaster and Merchant: An
Autobiography* (Salem, MA: Salem Press,
1921), 47–50; Susan S. Bean, *Yankee India:
American Commercial and Cultural Encounters with India in the Age of Sail 1784–1860*
(Salem, MA: Peabody Essex Museum, in
association with Mapin Publishing, 2001),
71–74; Dean T. Lahikainen, *Samuel McIntire: Carving an American Style,* (Salem, MA:
Peabody Essex Museum, 2007), 247–258.

INTRODUCTION—*THE ART OF WEDDING*

Paula Bradstreet Richter

People make art for many reasons. Art expresses some of humanity's most profound experiences — intellectual, emotional, aesthetic, spiritual, psychological, — in a seemingly inexhaustible variety of forms and media. Art provides a creative outlet for artists that both challenges and satisfies, expressing who they are as individuals or contributing to the cultural life of their communities. Encounters with art can be a lens through which individuals gain insight and understanding of people who lived in another time or place, and the world views, values, ideas, and struggles that affected their existence. The Peabody Essex Museum aspires to create engaging encounters between individuals and art that stimulate the mind, senses, and spirit and even transform perceptions, embrace new ideas, or reconsider familiar topics in surprising new ways.

This book and its associated exhibition, *Wedded Bliss, The Marriage of Art and Ceremony,* consider weddings as an impetus for the creation of art. They examine the creative impulses and artistic opportunities presented by various stages of the matrimonial process. The exhibition includes works by acclaimed international artists and also examples by highly accomplished artists or groups whose identities are not known. Art is a notoriously difficult concept to define. For the purposes of this exhibition and publication, a broad and open-ended understanding of art and artists is recognized and celebrated. The exhibi-

tion includes works by academically educated artists, by those trained through apprenticeship or through communal or familial transmission of knowledge and skills, by artists, designers, and craftspeople working in commercial and industrial settings, and by self-taught artists. These include some artists, such as the creators of dowry textiles, who have previously been marginalized in discussions about art. It includes works that may have a functional as well as aesthetic purpose, such as ceremonial objects. The exhibition has assembled a diverse array of artwork in many media including paintings, sculpture, works on paper, photography, film, clothing and accessories, jewelry, furniture, silver and metal ware, ceramics, mixed media, and contemporary art. Performing arts and certain forms of ephemeral aesthetic expression related to weddings, such as culinary or floral artistry, will be explored through programming held in conjunction with the exhibition.

The *Wedded Bliss* exhibition does not attempt to define weddings or marriage. It also does not propose to unify or order wedding rituals into a universal pattern or sequence of events. By organizing the exhibition thematically, it allows the viewer to consider parallel or divergent expressions of ideas, practices, or emotional responses, as embodied in art, that represent diverse aesthetic and cultural traditions. The exhibition is international in its focus with pri-

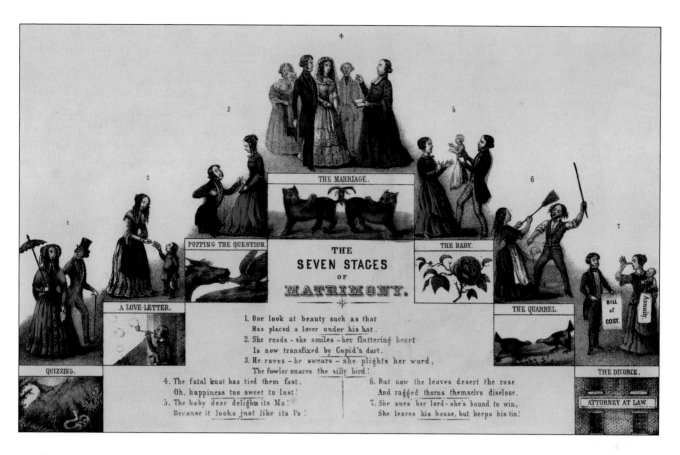

PLATE 5

Attributed to Nathaniel Currier (1813–1888) *The Seven Stages of Matrimony*, 1845 / New York / Lithograph / American Antiquarian Society, Worcester, Massachusetts

mary emphasis on the art of geographic regions and cultures that the Peabody Essex Museum typically collects: United States, China, Japan, India, Korea, Native America, Europe, Africa, and the Pacific region. While recognizing that it would be impossible to present an encyclopedic approach to this topic in an exhibition, it has been the intent to create meaningful comparisons between artwork created by international and American artists. While many works interpret aspects of the Euro-American "white wedding" tradition prevalent since the nineteenth century, a significant number of works explore the incredible diversity of art forms related to weddings in various locales around the globe. Each work is treated as the unique aesthetic expression of its maker, and the time, place, and circumstances for which it was made.

The temporal range of works in the exhibition spans the eighteenth century to the present. This time frame allows for exploration of art and ceremonial practices that occurred prior to the Industrial Revolution in the nineteenth century when many of the elements of the "white wedding" became formalized and codified. The consideration of weddings and art over the expanse of more than three hundred years challenges the concept of "tradition" as a fixed and static reality and suggests that traditions evolve and respond to forces of change over long periods of time. Even a cursory examination of historic wedding traditions that existed prior to or outside of the white wedding industry reveal how ideas about "tradition" have been manipulated and distorted for commercial purposes.

Several factors make an exhibition on the topic of weddings and art particularly relevant at the present time. Weddings are a phenomenon of contemporary American culture. In the last two decades fascination with weddings has grown exponentially in response to the burgeoning scale and lavishness of wedding ceremonies and changing views about marriage. At a time when the percentage of Americans that wed is declining, couples who do marry are creating ceremonies of unprecedented extravagance.

PLATE 6 (opposite)

Cile Bellefleur Burbidge (b. 1926)

Architectural Fantasy Cake, 2007 / Danvers, Massachusetts / Royal icing / Courtesy of the artist

Trained in fashion and clothing design, Cile Bellefleur Burbidge turned to wedding cake design while raising her children in the 1950s. Her long and accomplished career began with a class sponsored by the local YMCA. She developed a distinctive style of wedding cake that drew inspiration from architecture and from weddings of the Victorian period. Her cakes have been featured in the window display of Tiffany & Co. in New York, at Priscilla of Boston, and at numerous bridal fairs. *Architectural Fantasy Cake*, made especially for the *Wedded Bliss* exhibition, is a tour-de-force of cake design and demonstrates Burbidge's mastery of her medium— "royal icing," a combination of egg whites and sugar.*

*Vicki Howard, *Brides, Inc.: American Wedding and the Business of Tradition* (Philadelphia: University of Pennsylvania Press, 2006), 191.

PLATE 7 (top)

Mara Superior (b. 1951)

A Swan's Wedding Day, 2007 / Massachusetts / Ceramics and glass / Courtesy of the artist and Ferrin Gallery

PLATE 8 (bottom)

Mary Kawennatakie Adams (1917–1999)

Wedding Cake Basket, 1986 / Kahnawake Mohawk Nation, St. Regis, Quebec / Woven ash splint and sweet grass / Smithsonian American Art Museum

With the average cost of an American white wedding approaching $30,000, there have been many attempts in the popular and academic press to identify the factors that propel couples or families to expend such significant resources on a day or weekend-long celebration. It has also prompted studies of the consumer culture of weddings supplied by the vast industry of consultants, service suppliers, manufacturers, retailers, and marketers who use all available forms of media to reach their targeted audience. The fundamental purposes of the wedding as a marriage ritual are increasingly subsumed by forces that transform it into a vehicle for fashion, consumerism, and conspicuous consumption.[1]

The fairy-tale aspect of weddings has never been more pronounced. Celebrity weddings have become international media events promoted as ultimate expressions of contemporary fairy tales reported on by periodicals, tabloids, books, television specials, and the Internet. Not only does the wedding continue to provide the classic denouement of fables, fiction, films, and fantasies, it has taken on new relevance as the setting for situation comedies and reality television shows in which nuptial dilemmas, crises, and anxieties are performed for the entertainment of national audiences.[2]

Changes in marriage policy and practice in America have given new relevance to weddings as markers for societal change. Shifts in demographics, legal, and social policies have prompted changes in wedding practice. This has included new types of ceremonial observance as well as provided opportunities for artists to create works that explore the implications and intellectual and emotional responses that these changes

evoke. Increasing rates of divorce and remarriage have given rise to new customs, practices, and symbolic objects that recognize blended families. In recent years, the legal recognition of the marriage, civil unions, and commitment ceremonies of same sex couples by several states, including Massachusetts, has prompted the repurposing of historic traditions and creation of new practices and symbols that express gay and lesbian identity and the preferences of individuals involved. Ongoing political debate about gay marriage has also sparked the creation of art as an expression of protest.[3]

It should not then be a surprise that weddings have also been the subject of museum exhibitions. Several exhibitions in recent years have explored weddings from the perspective of fashion in displays that survey the extraordinary bridal attire worn at Euro-American white weddings and associated customs. A few exhibitions have considered international or ethnic wedding clothing, customs, and practices. Other exhibits have considered the topic through a particular medium, such as photography, or from the perspective of a particular time period. Each of these exhibitions has made contributions to the study of weddings that have provided a platform of scholarship on which this exhibition builds.[4]

The planning for this exhibition has benefited from scholarly review and dialogue with a group of exhibition advisors. Four of the exhibition advisors have also served as guest authors contributing essays to this publication. Two essays explore topics related to European and American art generated in response to marriage ceremonies, while the remaining three

PLATE 9

James Wells Champney (1843–1903) *Wedding Presents*, ca. 1880 / United States / Oil on canvas / Museum of the City of New York

essays focus on art related to international wedding traditions and attire.

The introductory essay, "Weddings, Creativity, and Art" examines the interconnections between weddings, art, and artists, through a consideration of the underlying creative impulses found in key forms drawn from the history of Western art and compared with selected examples from international artistic traditions.

In the essay "Wedding Rituals, Beliefs, and Arts," photographers Tiziana and Gianni Baldizzone draw on their extensive travels in remote regions of the world where they have participated in, observed, and created photographic art about marriage ceremonies. This essay considers how art is inextricably linked with ritual in cultures that maintain centuries-old traditions to the present day, often in spite of encroaching "globalization" and Westernized culture.

The essay "Wedding in White" considers the historical roots, aesthetic influences, and cultural significance of the Euro-American white wedding through its iconic symbols and visual expressions. One topic of particular interest is the meaning and evolution of the white wedding gown, introduced by Queen Victoria in 1840, and gradually adopted as the most prevalent form of bridal attire in the West.

Donald Clay Johnson explores how aspects of wedding dress and the creation of a ceremonial identity can be viewed as art in the essay "Wedding Attire." The essay also interprets the rich symbolism embodied in wedding dress from selected cultures around the world.

In the essay "Straightening Up: The Marriage of Conformity and Resistance in Wedding Art," Chyrs Ingraham explores how twentieth-century artists have used wedding-related subjects to question and critique taken-for-granted aspects of modern life and the culture of weddings. Her discussions of nuptial-themed art reveal the power structures that often underlie wedding iconography.

By examining weddings as the impetus for aesthetic expression and creativity, the exhibition, book, and related programs contribute to the dialogue about what constitutes art and how it is expressed by diverse artists working in many types of media. It is hoped that the exhibition will encourage the creation of new art and the continuance of ancient art forms and traditions including those threatened by modernity and the globalization of Western culture. The exhibition promotes the incorporation of art not only into significant rites of passage such as weddings, but also into the experience of daily living. Although weddings are a defining moment in life, they are not usually the end of the story but rather the beginning of a new chapter. The role of art in marriage is not the topic of this exhibition; however, sustaining a marriage over many years also requires artful creativity. As one eighteenth-century author advised young male apprentices, "though most men marry, few live happily; which manifestly proves that there is more art necessary to keep the affection alive...."[5]

ENDNOTES

1   Vicki Howard, *Brides, Inc.: American Wedding and the Business of Tradition* (Philadelphia: University of Pennsylvania Press, 2006), 108; Chrys Ingraham, *White Weddings: Romancing Heterosexuality in Popular Culture* (New York: Routledge, 1999, 4–5; 26–34; Rebecca Mead, *One Perfect Day: The Selling of the American Wedding* (New York: Penguin Press, 2007), 22–27; Cele C. Otnes & Elizabeth H. Pleck, *Cinderella Dream: The Allure of the Lavish Wedding* (Berkeley, Los Angeles, London: University of California Press, 2003), 2–5.

2   Sandy Schreier, *Hollywood Gets Married* (New York: Random House, 2002); Carol McD. Wallace: *All Dressed in White: The Irresistible Rise of the American Wedding* (New York: Penguin Books, 2004), 257–268.

3   Nancy F. Cott, *Public Vows: A History of Marriage and the Nation* (Cambridge, MA: Harvard University Press, 2000), 201–225.

4   "I Do: The Marriage of Fashion and Art," *IMA Previews* (Indianapolis, IN: Indianapolis Museum of Art, Summer 2006): 6–8; Grace Cohen Grossman, ed., *Romance & Ritual: Celebrating the Jewish Wedding* (Los Angeles: Skirball Cultural Center in association with University of Washington Press, 2001); Dorothy Ko and Valrae Reynolds, *The Bride Wore Red: Chinese Wedding Traditions* (exhib. brochure) (Newark, NJ: The Newark Museum, 2005); Charles L. Mo, *To Have and To Hold: 135 Years of Wedding Fashions* (Charlotte, NC: Mint Museum of Art, 2000); Barbara P. Norfleet, *Wedding* (Cambridge, MA: Carpenter Center for the Visual Arts, Harvard University, 1976); Gail F. Stern, ed., *Something Old, Something New: Ethnic Weddings in America* (Philadelphia: Balch Institute for Ethnic Studies, 1987).

5   *A Present for an Apprentice: or, a Sure Guide To Gain Both Esteem and Estate* (Philadelphia and Wilmington: J. Crukshank for James Williamson, 1774), 78.

PLATE 10

Nuptial Crown, ca. 1884 / St. Petersburg, Russia / Silver, diamonds, velvet / Hillwood Estate, Museum & Gardens

The practice observed by brides, and sometimes grooms, of wearing nuptial crowns is an ancient tradition found in many parts of the world, with notable expressions across Northern Europe. Nuptial crowns can be as simple as a wreath of orange blossoms or as elaborate as coronets made of precious metals and gemstones. Princess Alice of Hesse-Darmstadt, later the Empress Alexandra of Russia, wore this nuptial crown at her wedding to Emperor Nicholas II in November 1894 in St. Petersburg. Constructed of glittering diamonds, the nuptial crown reflects the skills of legendary court jewelers who fashioned jewelry and regalia for the Russian imperial family.*

Although the marriage of this imperial couple was reported to be one of mutual affection, their lives ended tragically during the Russian Revolution. Forced to abdicate the throne in 1917, Emperor Nicholas II along with his wife, their five children, and four attendants, were executed in July 1918. This nuptial crown was confiscated by the Bolsheviks along with other imperial jewelry and property, and was eventually acquired by an American collector, Marjorie Merriweather Post, who amassed an important collection of Russian art.

*Greg King, *The Court of the Last Tsar: Pomp, Power, and Pageantry in the Reign of Nicholas II* (Hoboken, NJ: John Wiley & Sons, 2006), 253–255, 343–355.

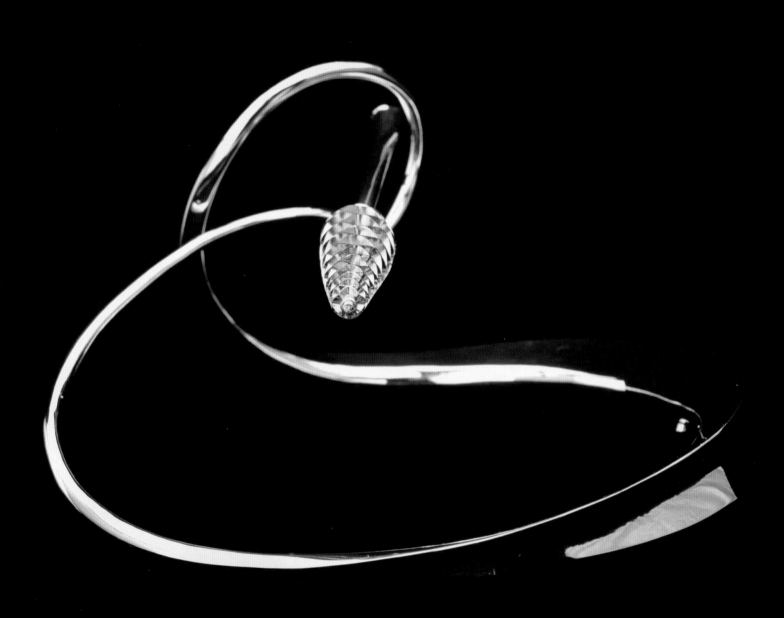

PLATE 11

Heikki Seppä (b. 1927)

Lupin Wedding Crown, 1982 / United States / Gold, silver, diamond / Smithsonian American Art Museum

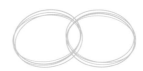

WEDDINGS:
CREATIVITY AND ART

Paula Bradstreet Richter

PLATE 13
William Hogarth (1697–1764)
*The Wedding of Stephen Beckingham
and Mary Cox*, 1729 (detail) / London /
Oil on canvas / The Metropolitan
Museum of Art

The act of wedding has been an impetus for the creation of art since antiquity. Art made for or about weddings can take many forms and be generated by a variety of impulses or intents. Wedding ceremonies have been documented by artists commissioned to record the occasion or who drew inspiration for their art from the dramatic pageantry of the event. For centuries, families and individuals have hired artists to create wedding portraits that depict the bride or the wedding couple at this pivotal moment in life.

PLATE 14

John Collet (1725–1780), Artist
Jabez Goldar (1729–1795), Engraver
Modern Love, PLATE I, *Courtship*, 1765 /
London, England / Colored line engraving /
The Colonial Williamsburg Foundation

PLATE 15

John Collet (1725–1780), Artist
Jabez Goldar (1729–1795), Engraver
Modern Love, PLATE II, *The Elopement*, 1765 /
London, England / Colored line engraving /
The Colonial Williamsburg Foundation

Barber traced the antecedents of fringed aprons worn with eastern-European ethnic and folk costumes during the modern era to archeological evidence of "string skirts," dating to the Paleolithic period, more than 20,000 years ago. These string skirts appear on Venus figures, Paleolithic sculptural representations of female forms that are among the earliest surviving examples of world art (figure 1).[2] Contemporary American artist Wendy Wahl found the string skirt a potent emblem of feminine identity and reinterpreted it as a feminist symbol of ancient origins and contemporary relevance (figure 2).

One does not have to venture quite so far back in time to find examples of
art associated with the preliminary stages of the matrimonial process. Artists
have found rich subject matter for artistic expressions in the romantic aspira-
tions and the emotional dilemmas involved in courtship and engagement. In
the West, courtship has involved the period prior to engagement or betrothal
during which individuals determine their inclination to marry, sometimes with
encouragement or negotiation of family members, matchmakers, or advisors.
Artists have made works that communicate intent or emotion related to court-

ship and engagement, that serve as ritual objects in premarital negotiations and betrothal, and that embody property exchanges related to marriage including bride wealth and dowries.

During the eighteenth and nineteenth centuries, ideas about courtship and how to find a spouse changed gradually in Europe and North America.[3] Completed in 1735, William Hogarth's painting *Marriage à la Mode 1: The Marriage Settlement* (figure 3) satirizes an arranged marriage between the son of an impecunious aristocratic family and the daughter of an affluent alderman in eighteenth-century England. Two fathers, with their lawyers, finalize the marriage arrangements while the couple sits at the left distracted by their own self-absorbed interests. The earl of Squander points to emblems of their bargaining, such as his family pedigree, while his grand but unfinished home can be glimpsed through the window. Symbols such as the chained dogs in the corner forebode an unhappy fate for the impending marriage. This painting was the first in a series of six related works that chronicled the formation and demise of an aristocratic marriage culminating in "a murder, an execution and a suicide."[4] Ten years later in 1745, the artist commissioned a series of prints based on the paintings that immediately became popular with international audiences. Satires of weddings and marriage were emulated by other artists, such as British artist John Collett's *Modern Love*, a series of four paintings painted in 1765 and later printed as engravings, that chronicle the courtship, elopement, honeymoon, and "Discordant Matrimony" of an ill-advised match (plate 17).

In contrast, American artist William Sidney Mount's *The Sportsman's Last Visit* (1835; plate 18) depicts an attractive young woman choosing between two suitors. The idea that young people, especially women, could make their own decisions about marriage based on personal inclination or romantic love was still a topic of considerable debate in the early nineteenth century.[5] Mount's painting offers wry commentary on the qualities of a prospective husband including education, professional and economic opportunities, and the romantic attraction between the couple. Winslow Homer's watercolor *Rustic Courtship* (1874; plate 19) suggests the challenges faced by individuals trying to determine their interest as prospective mates. Budding relationships face numer-

PLATE 19

Winslow Homer (1836–1910)

Rustic Courtship, 1874 / New England /

Watercolor and gouache on paper /

Collection of Mr. and Mrs. Paul Mellon,

Upperville, Virginia

ous obstacles including physical distance, compatibility, differences in family background, or social and economic barriers. Homer painted several paintings in the early 1870s on the topic of courtship that scholars now attribute to a period of romantic interest in the artist's life that ultimately ended in unrequited love.[6]

Exchanging love tokens in the form of miniature portraits dates back to the Renaissance. A rare and unique love token is Sarah Goodridge's *Beauty Revealed (Self-Portrait)*. Presumably a self-portrait by the accomplished Boston miniature painter, the tiny painting (plate 20) is an unusual expression of romantic interest and sexuality by a nineteenth-century American woman and artist. The miniature descended in the family of statesman Daniel Webster, whom Goodridge painted on at least a dozen occasions. Painted in 1828, Webster, aged forty-four, had been recently widowed and the forty-year-old artist is known to have visited Washington that same year. The surviving letters between Goodridge and Webster are suggestive but frustratingly ambiguous about the nature of their relationship, which continued over several decades. The couple did not ultimately marry, although Webster's family referred to Goodridge as his fiancée.[7]

"Popping the question"—the proposal of marriage—has been communicated by works of art. In 1758 or 1759, eighteen-year-old Benjamin West painted a miniature self-portrait (plate 21), framed it in a silver locket, and presented it with a proposal of marriage to Elizabeth Steele of Philadelphia. It is the earliest surviving work attributed to West, who later became an accomplished painter in London and a member of the Royal Academy. For centuries, miniature portraits had been exchanged as love tokens and West made use of this ancient convention for his marriage proposal. Sadly, his offer was declined although Miss Steele apparently kept the miniature in her possession.[8]

Since the late nineteenth century, the diamond ring has been the iconic symbol of engagement in Europe and America. A late-nineteenth-century etiquette book states, "Not long since, a solitaire diamond was almost universally selected for betrothals, its size varying according to discretion or taste."[9]

Other types of objects have been used as love tokens or to convey marriage proposals. Vermonter Ebenezer White, in 1782, carved a wooden busk for

PLATE 20

Sarah Goodridge (1788–1853)
Beauty Revealed (Self-Portrait), 1828 / Boston, Massachusetts / Watercolor on ivory / Metropolitan Museum of Art

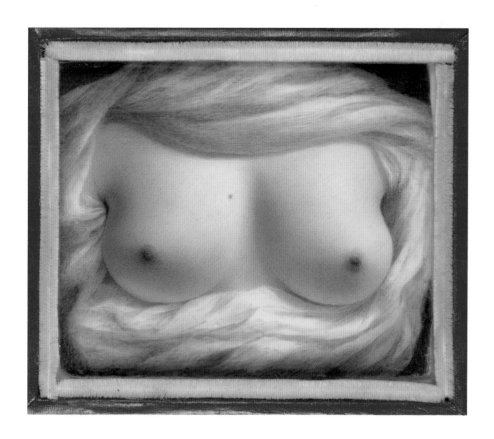

a woman's corset with the following verse: "IF U LOVE ME AS I LOVE U THEN I & U WILL MAKE 1 OF 2" (plate 22). This verse encircles two hearts that bear the initials *LP* for Lucy Packard, his intended bride. A busk was a rigid implement that slid into a vertical casing on the front of a corset to ensure good posture. Amorous decorations or verses on busks sometimes allude to physical intimacy with the wearer.[10]

In Japan, engagement traditionally has included the yuinō ceremony in which the groom's household bestows gifts on the bride's family. A gift of money to be used to set up the new household is accompanied by an array of ceremonial objects that have symbolic meanings (plate 23). Fashioned from braided paper cord covered in colorful foil, the figural emblems include the symbols of plum, pine, and bamboo signifying perseverance, longevity, and flexibility.[11] A crane and tortoise represent the hope for long life, and the spiny lobster suggests fertility and a marriage that lasts to old age.

Engagement is not always met with celebration. Art historians have interpreted Belgian artist James Ensor's painting, *Intrigue* (figure 4), created in 1911, as a response to criticism that neighbors leveled at his sister Mariette and her fiancé, Tan Hée Tsue, a Chinese art dealer, following their engagement. Ensor portrayed the couple surrounded by gossiping neighbors hiding behind masklike faces meant to conceal their biting commentary and ethnic and racial discrimination. The painting is considered one of Ensor's masterworks because of his enigmatic use of masks and the bold painting style that prefigures expressionism.[12]

Historically, preparations for weddings in many cultures have included property exchanges that provide goods or currency for the support of the new family and gifts or compensation to parental families for the loss of their

PLATE 21

Benjamin West (1738–1820)
Self-Portrait, 1758 or 1759 / Philadelphia /
Watercolor on ivory / Yale University Art
Gallery

PLATE 22

Ebenezer White
Busk, 1782 / Vermont / Carved wood /
Winterthur Museum & Country Estate

child and the child's contributions to the family economy. Property exchanges include creation of dowries, exchange of bride price or bride wealth, and gift giving. Objects associated with property exchanges often involve demonstrations of family or community identity, status, felicitous wishes, and generosity.

Bride wealth or bride price involves an exchange of material goods such as currency, animals, or other valued items between the prospective husband or his family and the family of the bride. When Europeans and Americans first encountered this practice they sometimes interpreted it as a form of purchasing a wife. However, anthropologists and ethnologists now recognize it as a complex system of social exchange that unites families in alliances meant to contribute to the stability of the marriage through material support, shared agreements, and values upheld by social

PLATE 23

Yuinō Engagement Gifts, 2007 / Japan / Paper cord, bamboo, balsa wood, metallic foils, glass, metal, plastic / Peabody Essex Museum

PLATE 24

Sophia Amelia Peabody (1809–1871) *Isola San Giovanni* [View of Lake Como, Italy], 1839–1840 / Salem, Massachusetts / Oil on canvas / Peabody Essex Museum

PLATE 25

Sophia Amelia Peabody (1809–1871) *Villa Menaggio, Lago di Como* [View of Lake Como, Italy], 1839–1840 / Salem, Massachusetts / Oil on canvas / Peabody Essex Museum

Following her engagement to aspiring author Nathaniel Hawthorne, painter Sophia Peabody created a pair of paintings as an engagement gift for her fiancé. The paintings depict scenes of Lake Como, Italy. Never having visited Italy, the artist drew inspiration from published etchings. She included a depiction of herself and her husband-to-be as small figures strolling arm-in-arm or embracing in the foreground of each painting, a romantic vision of their future life together. As emblems of deeply personal

sentiment, Hawthorne purportedly hid the paintings, covering them from view to protect their love from public scrutiny and comment. Following the couple's marriage in 1842, the paintings hung in Hawthorne's study in the Old Manse in Concord, Massachusetts.*

*Megan Marshall, *The Peabody Sisters: Three Women Who Ignited American Romanticism* (Boston: Houghton Mifflin, 2006), 403–407, 429–435.

networks. Ceremonial objects associated with this
practice are known in many cultures. A bride price
from Papua New Guinea (figure 6) includes the
kina, or gold lip, shell (*Pinctada maximums*) used
historically in monetary exchanges; in fact, it gives
its name to the modern currency of that country.[13]
For the Turumbu or Lokele peoples of the Democratic Republic of Congo in Africa, the institution of bride wealth is expressed in spear blade
currency, sometimes of very large size (plate 26).
These blades are considered a measure of wealth
and are not used as utilitarian objects. Blacksmiths
and metalworkers of central Africa are renowned
for their artistry in making specialized ceremonial
objects and functional implements in a metallurgy tradition that dates
back over a thousand years.[14]

The creation of dowries and trousseaux is another ancient tradition found
in many cultures. The dowry was typically supplied by the bride's family and
often included objects made by the bride and female relatives. A dowry was
intended to supply the new family with material goods, clothing, and resources
for their new home. Certain types of dowry items, notably textiles, were
often viewed as manifestations of the domestic skills, aesthetic tastes, and
accomplishments of the bride. Symbolic design motifs and patterns woven or

embroidered into these textiles embody cultural meanings passed down through generations. In recent years, as dowries become less prevalent in marriage practices—or even outlawed—textile scholars have researched and reinterpreted the significance of the aesthetic styles, symbols, and underlying meanings of dowry textiles.[15]

Typically made for dowries, suzanis are embroidered hangings and bed coverings from Central Asia (plate 27). The word *suzani* is derived from the Persian word for needle, and these textiles feature extensive embroidery in silk on cotton with elaborate floral motifs. Design influences were transmitted along the Silk Road, which extended from China to the Mediterranean. These large textiles could be used as coverlets for the marriage bed, wall hangings, or room dividers.[16] Another superb tradition of dowry textiles is found in the tapestries from the Scania region of southern Sweden (plates 28, 29, and 30). Featuring bold and colorful floral and figural motifs worked in dovetail or interlocked tapestry techniques, these textiles were used as bed coverings or chair- and carriage-cushion covers. Not only were these textiles displayed as evidence of the bride's domestic skills, they were also displayed during wedding processions and ceremonies, and later used to decorate homes for festive occasions.[17]

Examples of specialized furniture and containers created in association with dowry items and wedding gifts are known in many cultures and time periods. A remarkable example is the *Projecta Casket* (figure 7) dating from the late Roman period, ca. 380 C.E. A portrait of a couple surrounded by a wreath held by *erotes,*

FIGURE 6
Bride price, 20th century
Papua New Guinea, Highlands / Resin: tree; shell: mother of pearl; pigment: red ochre; fiber: pandanus leaf, cotton, knitted trade cloth; wood: bamboo / Fine Arts Museum of San Francisco

PLATE 26
Spear blade currency, 19th century
Lokele or Turumbu peoples, Democratic Republic of the Congo / Iron / National Museum of African Art, Smithsonian Institution

PLATE 27

Suzani, 19th century

Shahrisabs, Uzbekistan / Cotton, silk

embroidery / Minneapolis Institute of Arts

winged gods of love, appears in low relief on the lid of the silver-gilt toilet casket. Figures from Roman mythology ornament the sides of the casket along with a procession that may relate to a Roman bride's preparation for the marriage ceremony. Inscriptions suggest that the casket was a wedding gift to a Christian bride, Projecta, and Secunda, the groom, who likely practiced

PLATE 28 (left, top)

Floral Mosaic, Carriage Cushion Cover, c. 1800 / Sweden / Tapestry woven wool and linen / Khalili Collection of Swedish Textile Art

PLATE 29 (left, bottom)

The Annunciation, Carriage Cushion Cover, late 18th century / Sweden / Tapestry woven wool and linen / Khalili Collection of Swedish Textile Art

PLATE 30 (below)

Horses and Trees in Octagons, Bed Cover, 1830–1855 / Scania, Sweden / Tapestry woven wool and linen / Khalili Collection of Swedish Textile Art

traditional Roman religion.[18] During the seventeenth century, silver marriage caskets engraved with courting couples and emblems of love and matrimony were made in the northern Dutch province of Friesland. A groom from a noble or affluent family offered a marriage casket (plate 31), sometimes containing coins, to his prospective bride as a gift.[19]

Chests associated with marriage include forms such as a valuables cabinet made in 1679, the year that Joseph Pope (1650–1712) and Bathsheba Folger (1652–1726) of Salem Village, Massachusetts, were married. Attributed to the shop of joiner James Symonds of Salem, the applied spindles, elaborate moldings, carved ornamentation, and polychrome finish of this masterwork of New England colonial furniture emulated fashionable European Mannerist pieces (plate 32). The initials and date boldly carved into the plaque on the cabinet's door communicate the identity of the couple and the date of their marriage. In colonial America, textiles, ceramics, and silver, as well as furniture, were

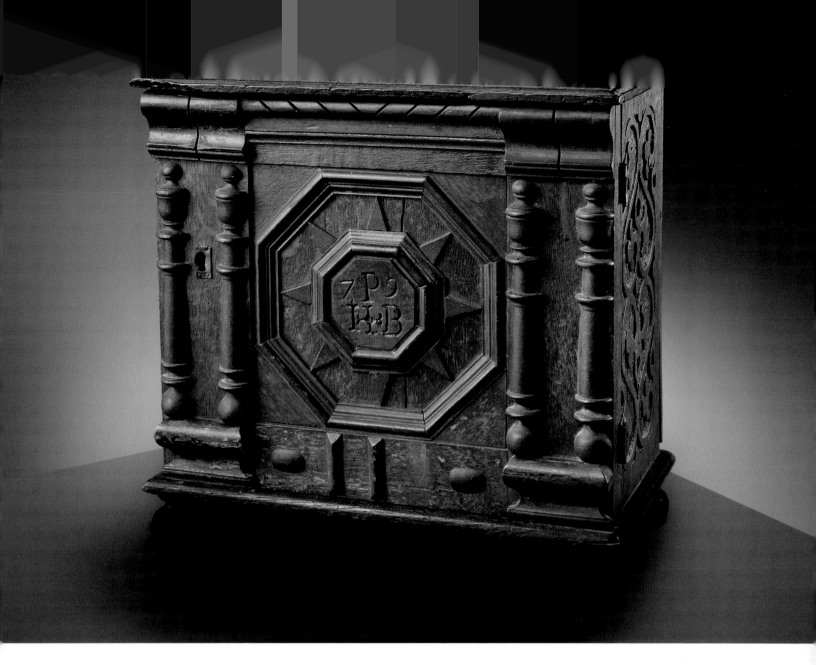

commonly marked with initials signifying ownership and documenting rites of passage such as marriage.[20]

Dowry and marriage chests served as containers for the goods and textiles that the bride brought into the marriage. Ivar Kvalen of Norway painted a large and sturdy wooden chest with colorful rococo scrolls and the initials of his daughter, Sirid, and the date of her marriage in 1777 (plate 33). Ornamental iron hardware and nailheads elaborate the decoration of the chest that she filled with her dowry linens, clothing, and valuables. In 1858, the bride's daughter and her family emigrated from Norway to the United States, bringing the chest with them to Wisconsin.

In 1935, Chou Lijuan brought a pair of wooden chests (plate 34) to her new husband's family home, Yin Yu Tang, in the village of Huang Cun, in the Huizhou region of Anhui Province in China. The marriage was arranged by the mother of Huang Zhenxin, the groom, with help from her sister, who lived in the bride's village. The couple did not meet until the day of their wedding. The chest is lined with brightly colored paper patterned with red roses. A

sheet of red paper glued to the lid bears inscriptions that list the dowry items that fill the chest. The family's home, Yin Yu Tang, was disassembled, moved to Salem, Massachusetts, and reassembled at the Peabody Essex Museum, where it opened to the public in 2003.[21]

PICTORIAL ART OF WEDDINGS

Weddings have been the subject of pictorial artwork dating back to antiquity and found in many cultures. Depictions of weddings have included works that explore the sequencing of ritual activities or events, the ceremony itself, and portraiture of the couple or the wedding party. Some of these works focus primarily on outward aspects of the event and the colorful pageantry involved with wedding ceremonies, but artists have also explored personal and emotional responses to these lively events.

The pageantry of wedding processions has long provided artists with a rich source of inspiration. In contemporary America, the wedding procession often consists of a short ride in a limousine and a quick walk down the aisle. However, this is not always the case in the past or in other cultures, where the procession is a distinct phase in the event, formalizing this moment of transition. Historically, the procession ritualized the moment of leave-taking, usually by the bride from her family. It also involved the transportation of the bride along with her dowry or personal possessions to the

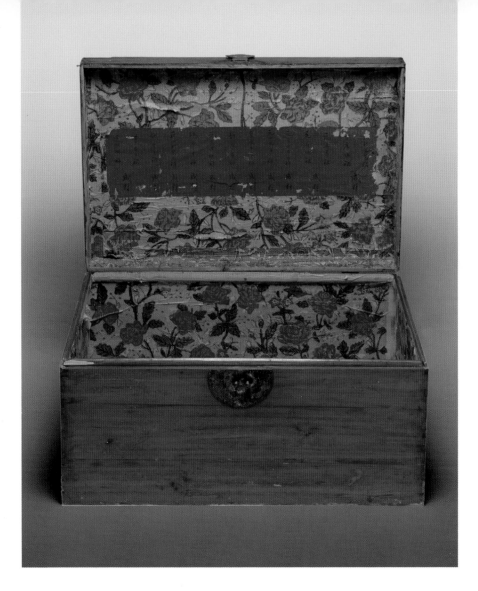

groom's home and the welcome
of the bride by the groom's family
prior to the actual ceremony. Processions are also an interlude when
the private ceremony intersects
with the public sphere as the bride
and the wedding party traverse
public thoroughfares on the way
to or from the ceremony.

*A Chinese Marriage Procession
and Country Views* is an album that
presents a series of twelve gouache
paintings recording multiple wed-
ding scenes from the early nineteenth century (plate 35). Chinese artists produced gouache paintings depicting everyday life in China for sale to European
and American traders at the port of Canton (Guangzhou). The pages of this
album bear a watermark of 1816 and handwritten pencil inscriptions provide
captions for several of the scenes. One painting depicts a "broker woman,"
a matchmaker or wedding advisor, being carried in a sedan chair. Ten of the
dozen images are devoted to the wedding procession, which includes musi-
cians, military figures bearing pikes, bearers of banners and decorative lanterns,
men carrying lavish displays of the dowry and wedding presents, and the bride
being transported in a lavishly ornamented sedan chair. The wedding series
culminates with two interior views depicting the bride and groom during their
wedding ceremony and the couple "asking a blessing of their parents."[22]

The rituals involved in royal weddings, including processions, are among
the most lavish and prescribed nuptial events. Royal weddings have never
been simply the joining of private individuals, but were state occasions that
established alliances between dynasties and nations. In *The Landing of Her Majesty Queen Charlotte at the Port of Harwich* (plate 36), British artist John Cleveley,
Sr., depicted German Princess Charlotte of Mecklenburg-Strelitz landing off
the coast of England on the way to her marriage with King George III, the

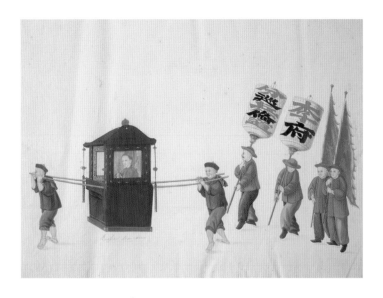

PLATE 35

Plates from *Chinese Marriage Procession and Country Views*, 1816 / Guangzhou, China, for the
Western market / Gouache on paper / Peabody Essex Museum

reigning British monarch. The painting depicts a wedding procession of the grandest scale involving royal naval vessels and hundreds of mariners and courtiers transporting the bride to her wedding ceremony. Seated under a canopy on a small barge at the center of the painting is the seventeen-year-old bride and her attendants, who were ferried to shore in the midst of a naval salute. The following day, the princess traveled by coach to London, met her husband for the first time, dined with his family, and then was dressed for the wedding ceremony that commenced at around nine in the evening. The ceremony was followed by a supper from which the couple retired between two and three in the morning.[23]

American impressionist Theodore Robinson immortalized the wedding procession in his painting *The Wedding March* (figure 8), which portrays prominent members of the international art community. On a painting trip to France in 1892, Robinson spent an extended sojourn in Giverny with the family of Claude Monet and other visiting artists. In July, Robinson attended the marriage ceremony of American painter Theodore Earl Butler (1861–1936) and Suzanne Hoschedé, the daughter of Monet's second wife. Robinson recorded in his diary that the wedding followed French marriage custom of a civil ceremony at the town hall (*le mairie*) followed by a religious ceremony at the church. In early August, Robinson commenced work on this painting, which captures his impressions of the bride, enveloped in a white veil, and the wedding party as it traversed the sunlit streets of Giverny.[24]

While the purposefully arranged space, elaborate rituals, distinctive dress, and emotionally charged atmosphere have made wedding ceremonies rich

PLATE 36 (top)
John Clevely, Sr. (1712–1777)
The Landing of Her Majesty Queen Charlotte at the Port of Harwich, 1762 / England / Oil on canvas / Anonymous loan

FIGURE 8 (bottom)
Theodore Robinson, 1852–1896
The Wedding March, 1892 / Giverny, France / Oil on canvas / Terra Foundation for American Art, Chicago

sources of inspiration for artists, the desire to document this important event has also prompted individuals and families to commission works that depict nuptial ceremonies or portraits of the wedding couple. Of special poignancy are works made by artists of their personal experience of weddings, of their own ceremonies, or of those with whom they share bonds of affection.

The hanging scroll *Preparations for a Court Wedding* (plate 37) features glimpses of the wedding party and their attendants engaged in activities prior to a marriage ceremony in eighteenth-century Japan. Behind the folding screen at the far right, an attendant bathes the groom's feet in a tub of water. At the center, the bride's kimono and dowry or gifts are displayed and admired by onlookers. In the lower scene, chefs prepare food for the wedding feast. Even elements of the landscape play a symbolic role. Felicitous symbols associated with marriage, such as the triad of plants—pine, plum, and bamboo—are expressive of longevity, perseverence, and resiliency. The pair of ducks, which mate for life, signify marital fidelity.

PLATE 37

Preparations for a Court Wedding, mid-Edo period, 18th century / Japan / Hanging scroll; color and ink on paper / Los Angeles County Museum of Art

Wedding portraiture of the nineteenth century and continuing into the modern era captured the idealized identity and appearance of the couple, particularly the bride, in their specialized wedding garb, at what was presumed to be the most elevated and pivotal moment in life. American painter Abbott Handerson Thayer (1849–1921) was noted for his ethereal portraits

PLATE 38
Abbott Handerson Thayer (1849–1921)
A Bride, ca. 1895 / New England / Oil
on canvas / Smithsonian American Art
Museum

52

and allegorical pictures of women and children. In Thayer's painting *A Bride* (plate 38), the figure is posed like an elegant statue with the pale tones of her clothing and the neutral background drawing attention to the serene expression and radiant complexion of her face. This unfinished work was a study for a commissioned bridal portrait.[30]

Russian-born painter Marc Chagall (1887–1985) returned to themes of love and marriage frequently during his long and prolific career. Perhaps more than any other artist of the twentieth century, he explored and exalted the rituals, traditions, and meanings of marriage in his work. In an early work, *Bride with Fan* (plate 87), painted in 1911, Chagall portrayed his fiancée, Bella Rosenfeld, whom he had left behind in Russia when he emigrated to Paris in 1910 to pursue his artistic career. While experimenting with the bold brushstrokes and semi-abstracted forms that characterize his early work, the twenty-four-year-old artist accoutered his beloved with white veil, flowers, and fan, creating a quintessential bridal portrait of the woman

FIGURE 12 (left)
R. B. Kitaj (1932–2007)
The Wedding, 1989–1993 / England / Oil on
canvas / Tate, London

PLATE 41 (opposite)
Amrit and Rabindra Singh
Nyrmla's Wedding II, 1985–1986 / England /
Poster paint, gouache, and gold dust on
mountboard / Courtesy of the artists

he hoped to marry. Four years after the completion of the painting, in 1915, the couple married when Chagall returned to his hometown of Vitebsk, Russia. The artist continued to portray his wife in his paintings throughout their marriage, which lasted until her death in 1945.[31]

In the twentieth century, artists have found the complex emotions evoked by weddings a rich vein of inspiration for portraiture. American artist R. B. Kitaj (b. 1932) created a bold and expressionistic depiction of his own wedding ceremony that compresses multiple impressions into a single narrative (figure 12). The artist began the painting six years after his wedding to artist Sandra Fisher in 1983. The couple's ceremony took place at the historic Bevis Marks Synagogue in London. Beneath the chupah, or wedding canopy, the artist leans forward to embrace the bride, whose face is partially obscured by his profile. The couple is surrounded by their three children, the rabbi, and several artists of the "School of London," who were members of the wedding party and friends of the couple. These included painters David Hockney, Lucien Freud, Frank Auerbach, and Leon Kossoff. The painting captures an autobiographical remembrance about an artist's wedding, an expression of Jewish identity and tradition, and an allusion to interconnections and friendships within the artistic community of London.[32]

Artists have also made images that rebel against the idealized and formulaic approaches to wedding portraiture in Western art. In *Nyrmla's Wedding II*

55

PLATE 42

Bikash Bhattacharjee (1940–2006)
Thakur Mathura Das, 1982 / India / Oil on
canvas / Peabody Essex Museum

(plate 41), British-Asian artist Amrit K. D. Kaur Singh created a family portrait in which she and her twin sister use henna to paint auspicious patterns, or *mehndi,* on the hands of the bride, their older sibling. The two women work individually and collaboratively in a style that they call "Past Modern," which draws inspiration from historic Indian miniature paintings integrated with elements of contemporary life and popular culture. Symbols of Western consumer culture and economic and environmental exploitation intrude into the peaceful interior scene and suggest how globalization threatens family, community, ethnic identity, traditional life ways, and values.[31]

In *Thakur Mathura Das,* painter Bikash Bhattacharjee (1940–2006) of Calcutta created an enigmatic depiction of two figures, a young girl dressed in bridal attire and an older man whose relationship to the girl is not clearly iden-

FIGURE 13 (left)
Marcel Duchamp (1887–1968)
The Bride Stripped Bare by Her Bachelors,
Even (The Large Glass), 1915–1923 / United
States / Oil, varnish, lead foil, lead wire,
and dust on glass panels / Philadelphia
Museum of Art

FIGURE 14 (right)
Max Ernst (1891–1976)
Attirement of the Bride (L'habillement de
l'epousée (de la mariée)), 1940 / France /
Oil on canvas / Peggy Guggenheim
Collection

tified (plate 42). This ambiguity leaves the viewer to wonder whether he is the groom, the father, or an unspecified acquaintance. In his work Bhattacharjee explored *shakti,* or cosmic energy, which is female, a force connecting women and goddesses in Hindu thought. The forthright gaze of the child bride projects an image of dignity and inner strength in the midst of circumstances and relationships that are uncertain and potentially ominous.[34] The subject of the painting raises the issue of child marriage, an ancient practice outlawed in India since 1929, though still practiced in parts of the world today.[35]

DRESSING THE BRIDE

Artists have been drawn to the potency of wedding attire as a cultural symbol and the ritualistic aspect of dressing the bride as a source of inspiration for their work. Not simply documentary depictions of bridal dress, these works explore a variety of topics including sexuality and the psychological or emotional responses to the act of wedding. In *The Trousseau* (figure 5), painted in 1910, American artist Charles Hawthorne (1872–1930) portrays a young woman being fitted for clothing prior to her wedding. The interplay of the figures suggests timeless activities of women equipping a bride for her new role as a wife, and also the mixed emotions of a young woman anticipating her impending marriage. The painting depicts more than the literal act of dressing; it suggests

the process of transformation that will alter the bride's identity and role in society as the result of the change in her marital status.

In *The Bride Stripped Bare by Her Bachelors, Even (The Large Glass)*, Marcel Duchamp (1887–1968) created a complex and enigmatic work that defies easy explanation (figure 13). As implied by the title, the work suggests the attempts by a group of nine "bachelors"—abstract shapes in the lower panel—to have an encounter with the "bride," a larger assemblage of geometric forms in the upper panel. The approach of the bachelors is impacted by mysterious mechanical devices creating a relationship of formal elements that art historians have interpreted as an allegory of forces that shape human sexual desire. Duchamp's creation of this work was meticulous in its conceptualization and in the skill used to create a complex assemblage from the unconventional materials. Its production stretched over eight years, from 1915 to 1923.

In a masterwork of Surrealist painting *Attirement of the Bride* (1940), Max Ernst exploited the theme of dressing the bride in a provocative and overtly sexual work (figure 14). The dreamlike scene features a nude bride partially clad in a red cloak and masked with an owl-like hood as she advances through an architectural setting. She is accompanied by a birdlike figure who carries a spear, a phallic symbol. Scholars have interpreted the bird-man as an alter-ego or emblem for the artist, which appears in a number of his paintings. It has also been suggested that the painting may refer to the artist's relationship with the young British artist Leonora Carrington, with whom he was involved until the couple was separated by the Nazi invasion of France in 1940.

Self-taught artist Brian White fashions fantasy sculptures from materials found on the seashore and in the hardware stores of Maine, his native state. In *Vintage White Dress and Veil* (plate 43), the artist created an "iconic representation of emotion and anticipation" that captures the romantic yearnings of men and women, voyages of the heart as echoed in the waves of the sea.[36] His sculptures blend the shell mosaics of nineteenth-century sailors' valentines with original interpretations of art, fashion, or popular culture that are transformed into metaphors or imaginary narratives about human relationships.[37]

SOLEMNIZING AND CELEBRATING

A wedding often involves rites that observe religious, spiritual, and ideological beliefs; legal and governmental regulations; formalized expressions of emotion; and community, family, and personal identity. Wedding ceremonies in many cultures require the creation or use of a ceremonial space set apart for the occasion and the use of ritual objects that serve as visual or tangible symbols of beliefs and values.

In many cultures, the wedding ceremony takes place in a space that has been specially prepared for the purpose, even if it is typically used for other functions.[38] Whether the wedding ceremony takes place in a home, a Las Vegas

PLATE 44

Goeseok Morando (strange rock and peony painting), 19th century / Korea / Eight panel screen, ink and color on paper / Peabody Essex Museum

wedding chapel, cathedral, synagogue, temple, Indian *mandap* or temporary altar, or Minangkabau *palaminan* or wedding alcove, there are many ways to demarcate ritual space and create the symbolic environment in which the wedding will take place.

Ritual artwork and objects play a role in defining the ceremonial wedding space and preparing it for use. During the Chosun dynasty (1392–1910) in Korea, weddings took place outdoors in a temporary area set up in a courtyard with a wood floor or platform on which the family arranged a folding screen, a table, and ritual objects. A wedding screen (plate 44) was painted with peony flowers in full bloom, symbols of prosperity, happiness, feminine beauty,

PLATE 45

Ricky Tims (b. 1956)

Shekinah (chupah or wedding canopy), 1995 /

Texas / Quilted textiles / Courtesy of

Dr. Isaac and Isabel Boniuk

love, and sexuality. This screen also features paired birds, symbols of marital fidelity. The wedding took place in front of the screen and, for the wedding night, the screen was moved to the nuptial bedchamber. So essential were wedding screens to Korean marriage rituals, that affluent families or government officials would lend them to families who could not afford to purchase these expensive objects.[39]

The Jewish wedding canopy, or chupah, provides a symbolic sacred space within which the marriage ceremony takes place. Originally a tentlike structure, the chupah can take many forms in terms of its dimension, shape, and aesthetic design. This gives opportunity for artistic expression and custom-

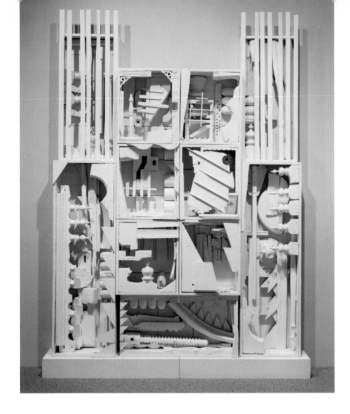

ized elements reflecting the tastes of the individuals involved. *Shekinah* (plate 45) by Texas quilt artist Ricky Tims, was commissioned in 1995 for use as a chupah. The title is the Hebrew word for "the radiant glory of God." The family who commissioned the work suggested the symbols—the dove of peace and the tree of life. The inscription in Hebrew, a biblical verse, predicts that the joyous voices of the bride and bridegroom shall be heard in the streets of Jerusalem.[40] The ritual space created for weddings has also served as the subject of abstract and pictorial artwork. Louise Nevelson's *Dawn's Wedding Chapel II* (1959; figure 15), suggests the compartmentalized space associated with ecclesiastical architecture such as cathedral façades or altarpieces. The sculpture is constructed from found objects, and the overall white paint unifies the elements into an abstract idea of ceremonial space. In its original form, the work included figures representing members of the wedding party. Contemporary Indian artist Dayanita Singh created a series of images—*Wedding Tents*—that explore the extraordinary constructions built for large weddings in India (plates 46 and 47). Singh creates architectural portraits of these dramatic but temporary structures, stage-

PLATE 70 (opposite)
Jacob Lawrence (1917–2000)
The Wedding, 1948 / United States / Egg tempera
on hardboard / Art Institute of Chicago

PLATE 71 (above)
Gari Melchers (1860–1932)
The Wedding, ca. 1892 / United States / Oil on
canvas / Albright-Knox Art Gallery

PLATE 72 (top)

Painted by Victor Eeckhout (1821–1879); made by J. Duvelleroy / Fan, "Moorish Wedding," ca. 1875 / Paris / Skin leaf, painted in oils; carved ivory sticks with gilt details; paste stone / Museum of Fine Arts, Boston

PLATE 73 (bottom)

Brisé Fan, ca. 1810 / Italy, possibly Russia / Silver filigree blades with silk ribbon / Museum of Fine Arts, Boston

Fashioned from fine silver wire, this fan features lacelike patterns in a technique called filigree. Design elements were formed by soldering the wire into motifs that include the fleur-de-lis, a rose, a heart, and a star. Silver filigree was produced in jewelry-making centers in Europe including Italy, France, and Russia. The provenance of this fan suggests that Emperor Napoleon I of France gave this fan to Marie Louise, Archduchess of Austria (1791–1847), who became his second wife in March of 1810. The couple married

first by proxy and in April held a wedding ceremony in Paris following her arrival in France. After divorcing his first wife, the Empress Josephine, earlier that same year, Napoleon sought a bride who could produce a male heir to the Bonaparte family and the French imperial throne and also strengthen alliances with ruling sovereigns of Europe.*

*Anna Gray Bennett, *Unfolding Beauty: The Art of the Fan* (Boston: Museum of Fine Arts, 1988), 218–219.

PLATE 74

Marriage Contract for Marriage of Esther Borgho and Abraham Borgho, ca. 1700 / Siena, Italy / Ink, gouache, and gold leaf on parchment / The Jewish Museum, New York

The *ketubah,* or marriage contract, is a document that has been made for Jewish wedding ceremonies since antiquity. Historically this agreement stipulated the groom's financial obligations to provide for the bride. It also documented the names of the couple, the place and date of the wedding, and was signed by witnesses. While the inscription on the document was determined by Jewish law, the artistic design of the contract allowed for aesthetic expression and creativity. Illuminated or illustrated ketubah feature motifs that reflect the influence of diverse artistic styles and cultural traditions. These designs include the family coat of arms at the top, two large figures representing Fame and Profit, the signs of the zodiac in the arch, biblical scenes including Adam and Eve, Jacob's Dream, and Moses at Sinai, and a variety of small genre scenes.

PLATE 75

Marriage Certificate of John and Elizabeth Blandin, ca. 1825 / Pennsylvania / Paper / Metropolitan Museum of Art

PLATE 76

Srilekha Sikander (b. 1950)

The Fisherman's Wedding, 1997 / India /

Watercolor on paper / Peabody Essex

Museum

WEDDING RITUALS, BELIEFS, AND ARTS

Tiziana and Gianni Baldizzone

PLATE 79

Tiziana and Gianni Baldizzone

Minangkabau Bride and Groom, 2001 /
West Sumatra, Indonesia / Tiziana and
Gianni Baldizzone

During the religious ceremony called the
nikah, the bride and groom listen to the
sermon by the *kadi*, or religious judge, and
speeches by the guests.

Beyond their religious and social dimensions, weddings are occasions for celebrating traditions. Since ancient times, weddings have provided rich opportunities for creative expression, putting artistry and creativity at the service of specific events and rites. This creativity must respond directly to the demands and needs of the bride and groom, their families, and the larger community or group to which they belong. Above all, it should help emphasize the aesthetic

each other; the butterflies embroidered on the festoons remind the bride how a virtuous housewife is like a butterfly who can make the community shine; the curling of a bud embroidered on a cushion tells how a father must raise his children and at the same time care for those of his sister; the tie-shaped flaps of material hanging from the canopy of the *palaminan* warn the spouses to choose their words carefully; and finally the silk curtains, which hang behind the nuptial seat in a number of layers that corresponds to the couple's social status, invite the couple to control their carnal instincts for many days before choosing to consummate their marriage. The *cerano*, a brass cup holding areca nuts, betel leaves, lemon, and the herb *gambir*, plays a central role in Minang-kabau weddings. When the young woman's family approves of the groom, and the wedding agreement is settled, the formal wedding proposal is presented in a ritual involving the dispatch of the filled-up *cerano* to the groom's home. While this sort of tradition is fast disappearing in many urban centers, the *cerano* continues to be used in the wedding ceremony itself to hold the acacia nuts and betel that are offered by the bride and groom to the guests.

A Minangkabau groom cannot enter the bride's house without the bronze bag holding the betel nut that he will offer to her mother. Likewise, for Niger's Peul Wodaabe, the wedding promise is accompanied by an inlaid and painted calabash, full of milk, which the groom's family gives to the bride's family to mark their commitment. In Tibet, bridegroom and guests are offered a welcoming *chang* (Tibetan alcohol) in a silver cup—silver being viewed as the purest of all metals. In Romania, among the Carpathian Maramures, the bridesmaids and other witnesses follow the wedding procession holding walking sticks adorned with red ribbons and bells, emblems of joy and fecundity.

JEWELRY AND RITUAL PARURES

Perhaps the most striking characteristic of wedding ceremonies in many traditional societies is the abundance of jewelry and ornaments. It is unthinkable for a girl to marry without jewelry: Wearing it brings good fortune. It shows how much the family cares for the bride and how much they have invested (sometimes becoming highly indebted) in her appearance for her wedding day.

PLATE 81

Tiziana and Gianni Baldizzone
Tibetan Nomad Bride, 1991 / Qinghai Province, China / Tiziana and Gianni Baldizzone

Tibetan bridal hairstyle made up of 108 braids adorned with a band of turquoises and coral.

A vast variety of parures and other specially crafted objects and accessories has emerged in response to different wedding traditions. They vary according to country, people, and community, and are often ascribed unique ceremonial meanings that make them irreplaceable. For many populations, jewelry and marriage parures represent more than simple bracelets and necklaces. Imbued with symbolism, they are worn for reasons that go far beyond the purely ornamental, expressing a particular vision of the world, a sense of belonging to a shared cultural model and an infinite range of possible beliefs.

Jewelry can have a variety of specific meanings, depending on the material used, the shape of the item, or the part of the body on which it is worn. It can, for example, be used to bless the union and bestow fertility and wealth. If a person does not own a suitable number of pieces, it is common to borrow them from relatives[8] or to rent them from professional jewelry lenders.[9] Notwithstanding the replacement of traditional materials with alloys or less-precious metals, or even plastic and synthetic stones,[10] the meaning and symbolism of specific pieces of jewelry can still rest intact.

Since ancient times and across virtually all cultures, gold's immutability, malleability, and rarity have made it the most sought-after metal for weddings. Hindus, for example, associate gold with the god Surya.[11] It symbolizes the sun and fire, and given its supposed purity is deemed the most appropriate metal for brides to wear on their heads, the purest part of their body. The Minang-kabau people of Sumatra, which was known in ancient times as the "Island of Gold," consider bracelets, necklaces, belts, and brooches in pure gold or gold plate to be not just important displays of wealth, but also an essential part of the *adat,* the complex of rules that since time immemorial forms the group's code of behavior, which it complies with even regarding details such as the choice of jewelry and clothing worn at a wedding (plate 79).

Associated in some cultures with the moon, the emblem of femininity, which is worshipped for its purity and light, silver is the second most popular material for wedding accessories and ornaments. The ancient gold and silver jewelry designs that continue to adorn the chests of Sami brides in Norway and Finland have long been imitated; copies have been found dating back to Byzantine times. In China's Guizhou province, people believed that silver offered protection against curses and attacks from the tigers that once infested the region's forests, and it continues to be associated with good luck today. Silver remains an important part of the wedding costumes of the Black Miao people, who continue to live in this region. The bride's hair is dressed with an elaborate crown of silver flowers surrounded by small engraved plaques from which hang myriad flower buds. The uppermost part of the bride's hair decoration resembles a bouquet of flowers in which peacocks[12] and other birds and butterflies rest.[13] Weighing more than twenty pounds and made by local Miao craftsmen, the array of silver necklaces, bracelets, pendants, brooches, and diadems forms a central part of the Miao woman's traditional wedding costume. The origin of such a massive use of silver jewelry among the Miao is still mysterious, so much so that it is typically explained through reference to legend[14] (plate 85).

Morocco's Berber people wear silver bracelets that are either twelve-pointed in shape or decorated with oblique lines. They are associated with weddings due both to their round, empty-centered form, which symbolizes femininity, and because silver is believed to protect the wearer from curses. In some Berber communities, there is an old tradition that is still continued today of letting a silver coin slip into the fiancée's slipper after the henna ceremony, for it is believed that silver, the so-called moon metal, will protect her from bad luck.

Likewise, both precious and semiprecious stones can possess highly symbolic connotations as part of traditional wedding jewelry. In Morocco, for example, pearls protect the wearer from bad luck. In Tibet and elsewhere in Himalayan regions, turquoise has the power to "absorb" sins and keep evil spirits at bay, and is considered a precious talisman since it represents the holy blue. Coral[15] is believed to bring good luck to the bride as its color symbolizes both good fortune and fertility.[16] Amber is seen as evoking the colors of the earth and is omnipresent in the wedding parures of Tibetan and Mongol women, and similarly is much appreciated among the Berbers as a result of its purported magical and healing properties. On their wedding day, Aït Atta women of Morocco traditionally wear necklaces of large amber beads that are handed down from one generation to the next, and symbolize sweetness and grace.

HEADDRESSES AND OTHER HEADWEAR

Almost everywhere, special care is taken with regard to the ornaments and accessories worn on the bride's and groom's heads. A particularly fine example are the *el jouhar*, the traditional pearl headdresses worn by the bride and groom that have made the craftsmen of Fez, Morocco, famous. The sumptuous costume, one of seven worn during the wedding presentation ritual, is worn by the bride, who displays it before the guests to elicit their approval and applause. It is so elaborate that the bride is unable to make even the slightest movement. Her body is completely enshrouded under a thick cascade of golden brocade, upon which the pearl headdress is placed. Seated cross-legged on a *mida* (a sedan chair), the bride is hoisted onto the shoulders of four Negaffats and carried off in procession during the *doura*, the final stage of the wedding ceremony, immediately before the bride and groom depart for their conjugal home. The pearls traditionally should have been bought during a pilgrimage to Mecca, and the parures that form the *el jouhar* are prepared during

PLATE 82

Tiziana and Gianni Baldizzone

Tamil Wedding, 2000 / Chennai, India /
Tiziana and Gianni Baldizzone

The ritual of the Kanyadhaan, at which
the bride's father gives her away to the
bridegroom.

Ramadan by the Negaffats, who are inspired by divine blessing brought on by fasting and prayers (plate 84).

Symbolic of beauty and perfection, immortalized by poets as the solidified tears of water nymphs,[17] pearls are believed to provide a formidable defense against evil and bad luck. It is for this reason that the most important points of a bride's body, such as her head and chest, are covered by pearls. A pearl and (synthetic) emerald necklace, known as a *selta*, embellishes her hairline; two bands of a large-knit net made of minuscule freshwater pearls, called a *zrair*, frame the face, while a drape made of baroque pearls held by golden loops and green stones covers the upper part of her chest. On the bride's forehead lays the *khit el rib*—the "line of the wind"—a pendant that represents the sealing of the wedding, when, at the end of the *doura*, the groom bends and kisses the bride's parure.

The *pöden*, the jeweled hairpiece worn by Tibetan brides, hangs from the head down to the waist in a cascade of amber, coral, and turquoise stones of every size. Among the nomads of the Tibetan provinces of Amdo and Kham, the wedding hairpiece consists of 108 very thin braids held together at the end by a large red or black band of velvet or cotton, onto which coral, turquoise (nowadays, mainly fakes), and silver studs are sewn. An ancient chant recounts that the woman wearing the braided hairpiece and the amber and coral *pöden* is a child born of decent and loving parents (plate 81).

Associated with weddings because of their sensual and inebriating smell, jasmine flowers are integral to the headwear of Tamil brides in Tamil Nadu, in southern India. Jewelry associated with marriage includes a *rakoli*—a round hair ornament made of gold, pearls, and rubies, and worn on the sides of the head only on the wedding day—and two hair clips representing Surya and Soma (the sun and the moon), which embody complementary opposites, the male and female elements, in memory of the first Brahmin marriage described in the *Rigveda* (plate 82).

The *suntiang*—the main headdress worn by Minangkabau brides—symbolizes the burden of responsibilities weighing on women in the Minangkabau society. About fourteen inches high and weighing approximately eleven

COSMETICS AS AN ART FORM

Wedding cosmetics provide another form of artistic expression that is filled with symbolism and meaning. The *bindior*—the red dot on the center of a Hindu bride's forehead—and the crimson powder (*sindoor*) that decorates the center parting of her hair are distinguishing marks of a married woman. Similarly, the deep red henna on the spouses' fingertips denotes the love between husband and wife, and hints at their sexual union. The henna on the Minangkabau fiancée during the pre-wedding *malam bainai* ceremony is an unmistakable sign that she has been promised to a man.

In Morocco many brides have between the eyebrows and on the cheeks and chin a series of blue, red, and white dots made of *aakar*,[19] forming either a triangle or a circle. These temporary marks shield the bride from the evil influence of the *djinns,* a mythical race of supernatural creatures. Perhaps the most spectacular form of courtship adornment is to be found among the men of Niger's Peul Wodaabe people. Here, free play is given to their innate aesthetic senses, resulting in masterpieces of pictorial facial art that serve but one purpose: seduction. In order to enhance the complexion's luminosity, they plaster their faces with *pura,* a yellow pigment coming from ochre fragments, and highlight the purity of their profile with a vertical line running from the forehead to the chin, drawn with *karmari,* an off-white paste. The whiteness of the eyes and teeth, signs of good health, is emphasized by kohl and carbon, which are used to darken the lips. At the annual *gerewol* parade of fiancées, Peul Wodaabe men made up in this way prepare to prove their endurance and *togu*—a mixture of charm and elegance—by competing against one another during so-called love dances in which they seduce and conquer young women who must choose a new husband or lover from among them (plate 83).

THE HENNAYA

In Moroccan wedding ceremonies, the henna day involves both Negaffats and the *maalma hennaya,* a henna artist whose wedding-eve task is to decorate the bride's hands and feet, which are deemed to be particularly exposed to demons and other negative forces. Henna, also known as the "plant of paradise," is ascribed magical and therapeutic powers and is an essential part of the bride's parure in many Far Eastern cultures[20] and in northwest Africa. The vegetable dye is seen as a tool of seduction that can also protect against curses and other evils.

The *hennaya* draws circles, curves, triangular arrows, and floral motifs into an intricate lace design that conveys a message, the meaning of which dates back to pre-Islamic times. Previously the *hennaya* used a small stick to paint the designs, but today it is customary to use a syringe. Among the symbols can be found the protective hand of Fatima, the hand being the natural instrument one would use to fend off an attack by something threatening. Thus the hand of Fatima is an Islamic motif that represents protection from evil. Fish, snakes, and frogs, which are thought to bring about fertility and serenity, are other symbols used by the *hennaya*. The henna ritual also involves the use of very elaborate gold-embroidered textiles, including the two cushions on which the bride's hands rest and the covers and cloths for the make-up dishes[21] (plate 84).

In front of the bride, on a small table covered by green tulle embroidered in gold with verses from the Koran, the Negaffat lays out a henna cup,[22] kohl for the eyes, and ampoules of rosewater and orange blossom water. Milk, honey, sugarloaf, and dates are added to these ingredients, each of them individual symbols of prosperity that can protect against malign influences, as do the incense, alum stone, and sandalwood scents that are kept burning in brass or silver censers along with bunches of mint and marjoram. Each of these ingredients is prepared according to ancient traditions.

WEDDING TEXTILES AND EMBROIDERY AS PAGES OF HISTORY

The Minangkabau Wedding *Songket*   The Minangkabau wedding ceremony is a joyous combination of tradition and art: Everything is *adat*, not just the rituals but also the ornamental accessories. The decorative motifs used represent the transposition onto textile of the Minangkabau's basic philosophy of life, perhaps best captured in the saying "Nature is our teacher." This aphorism is the key to understanding the designs and images that cover the textiles and embroideries associated with marriage among these people, who make each piece both unique and an integral part of their cultural heritage. Weaving and embroidery are taught from early childhood and are skills that every mother passes to her daughters. Indeed, being able to weave and embroider is an essential requirement for any would-be bride.

While there is a growing trend in Indonesia for brides to marry in Western-influenced white wedding dresses and tulle veils, Minangkabau brides, whether simple agricultural smallholders or successful international businesswomen, continue to marry swathed in lavish *songkets*. The weavers from Pandai Sikek, a textile center near Bukkitinggi, refer to the *songket* as the "skin of the *adat*." Four golden stripes represent the qualities required of all Minangkabau women: serenity, wisdom, frugality, and the skill to manage the land and home efficiently. Bamboo, represented by an isosceles triangle, symbolizes the three men to whom the preservation of culture is assigned: the *pangulu*, who is responsible for the *adat*; the *ulama*, the spiritual leader responsible for the teaching of Islamic principles; and the *cadiak pandai,* the wise man who plans the future of the village. The *itiak pulang patang*—a series of oblique, intertwined *S*-es representing ducks returning home in the afternoon—provides a warning to the wearer not to forget one's maternal home,[23] while a diamond-shaped design symbolizes the *galamai*—the wedding cake—itself a symbol of the sweetness of an *adat* marriage.

The Embroideries of the Black Miao Brides in Southwest China

Embroidery represents the principal means by which the Miao people of China communicate their history. More than a thousand years ago, Miao brocades were already famous among the Chinese of the Tang dynasty. Today they still constitute the primary reference works for scholars seeking to understand the legends and history of the Miao. According to tradition, the brocade costume should be embroidered by the same person who wears it, and it is deemed a woman's most effective weapon of seduction in her search for a future husband. Until recently, a young Miao woman who could not embroider was destined to remain single, as Miao tradition determined that a man should select a bride on the basis of her brocade, and it was therefore no coincidence that once a man's courtship

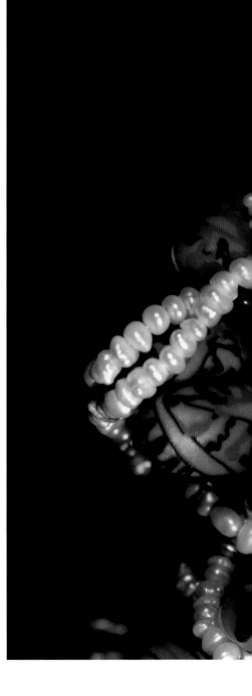

PLATE 84

Tiziana and Gianni Baldizzone

Fassi Wedding, 2000 / Fez, Morocco /
Tiziana and Gianni Baldizzone

The pearls of the bridal parure are bought
during a pilgrimage to Mecca.

advances had been accepted, he would receive a strip of the embroidered fabric to
be used in the would-be bride's wedding dress.

For centuries, young Miao girls have been taught the art of embroidery
from early childhood, and by the age of ten or twelve know by heart the full
range of flat stitch, cross stitch, or chain stitch techniques required. Many
of today's younger generation, however, no longer have the time to learn the
art of embroidery—they are often more familiar with the computer than
with needle and thread—and, as a result, their wedding dresses are increasingly assembled from machine-made fabric and embroideries, with a value far
removed from those made in remote villages by mothers and daughters according to traditional methods and techniques. These women, combining the
practical need to make the fabric thicker in order to protect those areas of the

fabric most prone to wear-and-tear (such as the hems of the sleeves) with an age-old knowledge, record on the wedding dress the mythology, legends, and history of the Miao people. A plait denotes the crossing of a river, a piece of zigzag embroidery indicates the winding paths in the Leigong Mountains, and a hem on the sleeve cuff symbolizes the Yellow River, the region from which the Miao people come. Sacred and auspicious creatures such as the scolopendra (a giant centipede) and the mythical phoenix alternate with dragons, dragonflies, butterflies, and fish,[24] and all of these frame the feats of the heroine Wu Moxi, who, so tradition says, at times of war and battle, scatters seeds that are transformed into warriors ready to fight alongside the Miao people (plate 85).

VANISHING TRADITIONS

Many wedding traditions are disappearing along with the accessories and creations with which they are associated. This is happening for a number of reasons. In some instances, for example, historic practices and ways of doing things have simply faded into obscurity and the objects associated with them have become nothing more than antiques,[25] while in other cases, external influences have engendered new traditions[26] that have replaced seemingly outdated local traditions with new, more fashionable ones from outside the society or culture (plate 86).

Ever more frequently, we find that when we ask spouses why they wear a particular piece of jewelry or headwear, their answer is the same: "Because it is our custom." Often, only older people are still aware of the original meanings of these various wedding accessories and why they are worn. Indeed, there have been times when, as a result of having read specialized scientific papers on the subject, it seems that we know more than local people about the specific meanings and histories associated with these accessories and ornaments, as their origins have become lost and disconnected from the wedding ceremonies themselves.

Aside from the disappearance of these rituals, customs, and related accessories, we have also detected a worrying decline in creative capacity, which is having significant consequences on the quality of many of the objects that continue to be used at weddings. This process of decline is by no means unique to weddings, but instead affects craftsmanship in general. For the case of weddings, it can be largely explained by the fact that, until relatively recently, it was the responsibility of brides and their families, or at least craftspeople from the same ethnic or cultural group, to prepare the parures, trousseaux, and other accessories used at the wedding. The personal and direct involvement of these people in the creative process ensured high standards of artisanry and quality. Sadly, this is no longer the case, for the rhythms of everyday modern living have been transformed, even in the remotest of rural areas. As a result, girls and young women no longer have the requisite time—sometimes measured in years—to embroider, weave, and sew bridal gowns and elaborate wedding trousseaux. Families now spend their scarce resources on low-cost consumer durables[27] rather than the hand-stitched blankets and embroidered rugs of bygone times. Similarly, craftspeople are compelled to put quantity and price before quality and pride, sacrificing skill and sensitivity to the demands of speed and economy. The true cost of these changes is far higher than it may seem, for we are now bidding farewell to a rich and irreplaceable heritage of traditional know-how and creativity.

A glimmer of hope remains.[28] In some communities, where ties with tradition remain strong,[29] there is a growing tendency for people who have emigrated away to return to their original communities to celebrate their marriages in line with historic traditions. In such instances, the wedding functions as a social "moment," emphasizing the sense of belonging and reinforcing ties among individuals and the groups and communities to which they belong. Inversely, in other instances, and in the interests of fashion, display, or even nonconformity, some couples may choose styles of wedding and related traditions that are quite distinct from those indigenous to their own backgrounds, thereby supporting a process that, unbeknownst to them, can contribute directly to the survival of these traditions and the craftsmanship with which they are associated, which otherwise would be destined to disappear.[30]

PLATE 86

Tiziana and Gianni Baldizzone

Kazakh Couple in Their Yurt, 2005 / Mount Altai, Xinjiang Province, China / Tiziana and Gianni Baldizzone

A Kazak woman in her yurt with the photograph of her and her husband's "white wedding."

ENDNOTES

1   Well known in Fez for the last couple of centuries, the Ben Cherif weavers have extended their fame well beyond Moroccan borders, gaining recognition in France since the first half of the nineteenth century, and in the United States—where they sold their textiles in a Boston outlet at the start of the twentieth century. Always keeping an eye on the market, they began buying new jacquard looms in order to modernize their stock, therefore beginning the transition that is still going on today by newer generations, many of whom are now qualified in textile engineering.

2   The technique involves adding a silver and gold thread to the basic textile. The weavers must count the weft threads before they spin the spool or spools holding the supplementary thread to obtain the negative-positive motifs that characterize this style of textile.

3   Today, the craftsmen from this village have no other choice but to use the same poor-quality materials used in other areas. These flat and shiny threads deprive pieces of their intrinsic beauty, turning them into kitsch products, and eliminate regional characteristics and differences. Nowadays, since the textiles tend to be made from the same basic materials, they all tend to look exactly the same.

4   A similar role is held in West Sumatra by the professional women in charge of organizing the Minangkabau weddings. Families resort to them to dress the bride and groom. These women know all the rituals and own all the ornaments required by tradition. Their primary role is to dress the bride and groom to perfection in order to guarantee the success of the subsequent *adat* ceremony.

WEDDING IN WHITE

Paula Bradstreet Richter

PLATE 87

Marc Chagall (1887–1985)
Bride with Fan, 1911 / Paris, France / Oil on
canvas / Metropolitan Museum of Art

With roots that can be traced to the mid-nineteenth century, the white wedding is a formulaic approach to wedding that has become a prevalent form of marriage ceremony in American society. Sociologist Chrys Ingraham has described the white wedding as "a spectacle featuring a bride in a formal white wedding gown, combined with some combination of attendants and witnesses, religious ceremony, wedding reception, and honeymoon."[1] In its visual expression the white wedding is comprised of a series of iconic emblems: a diamond engagement ring, a white wedding dress and dark tuxedo, a white wedding cake, a set

of matching champagne flutes, a white limousine, and wedding bells. Around these swirl a series of milestone events and gestures that signify the matrimonial process: proposals or "popping the question," bridal showers and bachelor parties, wedding processions, Mendelssohn's "Wedding March," a religious or secular commitment ceremony, kissing the bride, tossing the bouquet, a lavish reception, throwing flower petals or grain at the departing couple, and decorating the newlyweds' vehicle with signs, tin cans, and old shoes prior to their departure for a honeymoon in an exotic destination.

Combining ancient practices with newly fabricated and commercialized traditions, the white wedding has increasingly evolved into an extravaganza of conspicuous consumption supplied by a vast industry comprised of manufacturers, retailers, news and entertainment media, and service providers. Originally rooted in nineteenth-century Christian religious and ceremonial practices, the white wedding has been found to be adaptable to secularization or to blending with other faiths and cultural traditions. Once practiced

PLATE 88 (left)
Advertising Art Photograph for Priscilla of Boston, ca. 1970 / Boston, Massachusetts / Gelatin silver print / Peabody Essex Museum

PLATE 89 (right)
Advertising Art Photograph for Priscilla of Boston, 1955 / Boston, Massachusetts / Gelatin silver print / Peabody Essex Museum

primarily in Europe and North America, the influence of the white wedding is now felt in many parts of the world.[2]

Artists have responded to the white wedding both by creating original artwork that complies with its conventions or by working outside of its strictures as a means of protest or commentary. Some of the artwork featured in *Wedded Bliss* draws on the visual symbols and aesthetic traditions of the white wedding making it relevant to consider the historic context that gave rise to this approach and the ways in which it is manifested in American culture of the nineteenth and twentieth centuries.

Many scholars trace the roots of the Euro-American white wedding to the marriage of Queen Victoria of Great Britain and Prince Albert of Saxe-Coburg and Gotha that took place on February 10, 1840. Three years earlier, in 1837, the bride ascended to the British throne at the age of eighteen. Her impending marriage had been the subject of much speculation and her engagement to the tall German prince appealed to romantic imaginations around the world.[3]

PLATE 91

Cameo Parure, ca. 1820 / Italy / Gold,
shell, brass, leather, silk / Peabody Essex
Museum

In 1822 Jane Appleton Peele (1802–1837)
of Salem, Massachusetts, received this
cameo parure, or matching set of jewelry,
from her husband, Stephen Phillips, on
the occasion of their wedding. The scenes
carved in the shell cameos depict ancient
Greek and Roman mythological subjects.
The earrings feature a quiver of arrows
crossed by a cupid's bow, a symbol of love
and marriage. The belt buckle displays allegorical figures of Day and Night, adapted
from the works of Danish neoclassical
sculptor Bertel Thorvaldsen (1770–1844).
Italian cameo carvers sculpted the intricate
scenes by hand into conch shells that were
then fitted into gold settings by jewelers.*

*Martha Gandy Fales, *Jewelry in America,
1600–1900* (Woodbridge, Suffolk: Antique
Collectors' Club, 1995), 127.

aristocracy, and high-profile families, and on the increasingly lavish celebrations
associated with the Belle Epoque. Audience interest in, and media reporting
on, celebrity weddings intensified in the twentieth century. Print media and the
expanding film and television industries covered royal marriage ceremonies such
as that of the young Princess Elizabeth—now Queen Elizabeth II—to Prince
Philip Mountbatten in 1947, or film star Grace Kelly's marriage to Prince Rainier
of Monaco in 1956. These prefigured the ultimate nuptial spectacle of the twentieth century, the wedding of Lady Diana Spencer to Charles, Prince of Wales,
in July 1981, which was watched by an international television audience of 750
million people. This event renewed interest in the formality, splendor, and privi-
lege associated with the white wedding and reinforced associations with fairy-tale
romances and brides who became princesses on their wedding day.

The entertainment industry has also promoted the white wedding in films
and television programs that, although fictional, have had significant impact
on disseminating ideas about weddings and marriage. Whether in classic films
or recent box office hits, movies and television programs have showcased weddings as "happy endings" worthy of elaborate celebrations. They have also
provided audiences with information on the latest fashions in wedding dresses
and set expectations about norms for the wedding ceremony and the matrimonial process that equate marriage with the proverbial adage ". . . and they lived
happily ever after."

While considering art made for or within the white wedding tradition,
Wedded Bliss also offers alternatives drawn from the American past and present
and through comparisons with non-Western cultures. The intent of this is not
to disparage the white wedding or downplay the significant creativity and artis-

PLATE 92
Seed Pearl Parure,
ca. 1845 / United States / Seed pearls,
mother-of-pearl, gold, silk, leather, wood,
cardboard / Peabody Essex Museum

tic expression found within this tradition, but to suggest that there have always been other approaches to art and ceremony that are equally rich in aesthetic and cultural meaning. It is hoped that the artistic and intellectual dialogue posed by these comparisons of diverse traditions will encourage artists to find new inspiration in the topic of weddings and will enrich the experience of couples who plan future weddings through the inclusion of art in their marriage ceremonies.

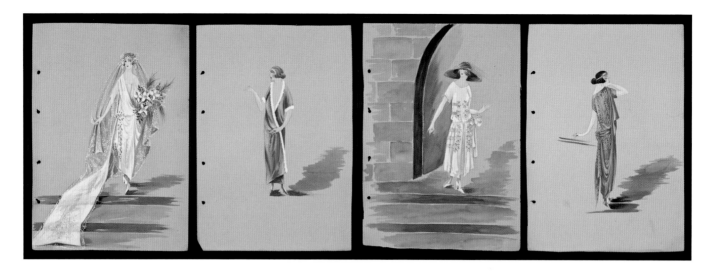

ENDNOTES

1   Chrys Ingraham, *White Weddings: Romancing Heterosexuality in Popular Culture*. (New York: Routledge, 1999), 3.

2   Cele C. Otnes and Elizabeth H. Pleck, *Cinderella Dreams: The Allure of the Lavish Wedding*. (Berkeley: University of California Press, 2003), 197–227.

3   Shelley Tobin, Sarah Pepper, and Margaret Willes, *Marriage à la Mode: Three Centuries of Wedding Dress* (London: National Trust, 2003), 32–33.

4   "Marriage of the Queen," *Haverhill Gazette* [*Essex Gazette*], vol. 4, no. 11 (March 14, 1840): 2.

5   Nigel Arch and Joanna Marschner, *Royal Wedding Dresses from the Royal Ceremonial Dress Collection at Kensington Palace* (London: Historic Royal Palaces, 2003), 4–7; Ingraham, *White Weddings*, 34–35, 52; Otnes and Pleck, *Cinderella Dreams*, 30–32; Tobin, Pepper, and Willes, *Marriage à la Mode*, 32–33; Carol McD. Wallace, *All Dressed in White: The Irresistible Rise of the American Wedding* (New York: Penguin Books, 2004), 32–35.

6   Rebecca Mead, *One Perfect Day: The Selling of the American Wedding*. (New York: Penguin Press, 2007), 76.

7   Elizabeth Johns, *American Genre Painting: The Politics of Everyday Life* (New Haven: Yale University Press, 1991), 147–151; Justin Wolff, *Richard Caton Woodville: American Painter, Artful Dodger* (Princeton: Princeton University Press, 2002), 158–175.

8   Mrs. John Sherwood, *Manners and Social Usages* (New York: Harper & Brothers, 1897), 82.

9   Ibid., 84.

10   Vicki Howard, *Brides, Inc.: American Weddings and the Business of Tradition* (Philadelphia: University of Pennsylvania Press, 2006), 114–121; Wallace, *All Dressed in White*, 193–195.

PLATE 93

Maison Ruffie

Mariage de Mademoiselle Lucie Wheatland, 1921 / Paris / Watercolor and gouache on paper / Peabody Essex Museum

When American bride Lucia Pickering Wheatland married in 1923, she had her bridal gown and trousseau designed by the Parisian dressmaking firm of Maison Ruffie. The firm created an album of original sketches of the wedding gown, day and evening dresses, and lingerie that depict the elegant styles worn by a fashionable bride in the early twentieth century.

PLATE 94

Wedding Dress, 1719 / Cambridge, Massachusetts / Silk with reproduction petticoat and accessories / Peabody Essex Museum

White wedding gowns did not become standard for bridal attire in America until the late nineteenth century. During the colonial period, brides wore fashionable dresses in a variety of colors made from imported fabrics. One of the earliest surviving wedding gowns from colonial America is the dress worn in 1719 by Mary Leverett (1701–1756). It is made of yellow silk satin with weft patterning of exotic floral motifs woven in bands of blue, coral, and green. The imported British silk may have been woven approximately ten years prior to the wedding. Like many eighteenth-century dresses, the garment was altered at a later period and originally may have had a more voluminous silhouette, possibly in the form of a mantua, or loosely fitted gown with draped skirt worn over a petticoat. The bride was a descendant of Governor John Leverett of Massachusetts, and her father was the president of Harvard College.*

*Charles Edward Leverett, *A Memoir Biographical and Genealogical, of Sir John Leverett, Knt., Governor of Massachusetts 1673–79; of Hon. John Leverett F.R.S., Judge of the Supreme Court and President of Harvard College; and of the Family Generally* (Boston: Crosby, Nichols, and Company, 1856), 145–147; Natalie Rothstein to Paula Richter, March 5, 1998, American Decorative Art department files, Peabody Essex Museum; Consultation with costume historian, Nancy Rexford, January 2008.

PLATE 95

Wedding Dress, 1837 / Boston, Massachusetts / Silk, cotton, metal / Peabody Essex Museum

The dressmaker's artistry is demonstrated by the elegant silhouette, shimmering fabric, and intricate pleated details on the bodice and sleeves of this white satin wedding gown. The original owner of the dress, Mary Copley Greene (1817–1892), married James Sullivan Amory (1809–1884) in Boston on November 27, 1837. The bride was a granddaughter of the American painter John Singleton Copley (1738–1815).*

*The Greene Family of England & America with Pedigrees (Boston: Privately printed, 1901), 55–56, 74.

PLATE 96

Wedding Dress and Necklace, 1872 / North Shore, Massachusetts / Dress: Silk, cotton, metal; Necklace: Stone beads / Peabody Essex Museum

Although white wedding gowns were promoted by fashion magazines following the example of Queen Victoria, many brides in the late nineteenth century chose to wear dresses of other colors for practical or personal reasons. The cost of creating a pure white dress to be worn only once was prohibitive, and many brides created a stylish dress in a fashionable color that could be worn as their "best dress" for some time after the wedding. Jeanette Renton selected a bright blue silk for the dress worn to her marriage ceremony to Frank Cutts, in May 1870. The dress is constructed in three pieces including a bodice, skirt, and overskirt and is accompanied by a white beaded necklace with cross-shaped pendant. The dress features bands of elaborate trimming in the shape of interlocking hearts, which are machine-stitched from the blue silk fabric.

PLATE 97

Wedding Dress, 1865 / Massachusetts / Silk, cotton, other materials / Peabody Essex Museum

When Massachusetts bride Ellen B. Hayden (1838–1897) married in February 1865, the United States had been embroiled in the Civil War for almost four years. The war had an impact on the lives of Americans in many ways and even influenced fashionable dress of the period. The design of this gown was likely modeled on an illustration published in the January 1865 *Godey's Lady's Book,* a popular women's magazine. The bands of trim at the shoulders emulate epaulettes and shoulder bars of military uniforms.* The gown features two bodices: one with a low cut neckline for evening wear (opposite) and a more modest bodice for the daytime ceremony (above). The bride was the daughter of the Lieutenant Governor of Massachusetts and the wedding took place at Williamsburg, Massachusetts, near her hometown. She married Solomon Lincoln (1838–1907), a young lawyer from Salem, Massachusetts.†

*Godey's Lady's Book and Magazine, vol. 70 (January 1865): 1st color plate.

†Waldo Lincoln, *History of the Lincoln Family: An Account of the Descendants of Samuel Lincoln, of Hingham, Massachusetts, 1637–1920* (Worcester, MA: Commonwealth Press, 1923), 446–447.

PLATE 98

Wedding Dress, 1880 / Massachusetts / Silk, wax, cotton, metal, glass, other materials / Peabody Essex Museum

This elaborate wedding ensemble with bustle and train exemplifies the taste for surface ornamentation, draping, and pleating that was popular in the 1880s. The dress retains its original trim consisting of intricate bands of imitation pearls and sprays of orange blossoms made of wax, fabric, and wire. The fragrant white flowers were worn by Queen Victoria at her wedding in 1840 and were prized by nineteenth-century brides for their symbolic association with purity and chastity. This dress was worn by Alice Poore (1854–1883) who married financier Frederick S. Moseley (1852–1938) on September 29, 1880, in West Newbury, Massachusetts.

PLATE 99

Peggy Hoyt, Inc.

Wedding Gown and Accessories, 1931 /
New York / Silk and other materials /
Peabody Essex Museum

The dressmaking firm founded by
American designer Peggy Hoyt (1893–1937)
advertised as "Milliners, Dressmakers and
Tailors to the American Aristocracy." The
firm catered to an affluent and influential
clientele and was well known for elegant
gowns, accessories, and also theatrical
costume designs. When planning her
wedding in 1931, Sally Parker (1907–2000)
selected Hoyt to create an elaborate bridal
ensemble. (Sally Parker was the daughter
of George S. Parker, who founded the
game manufacturing firm Parker Brothers.)
Made of white silk satin cut on the bias to
create flowing drapes of fabric, the dress
features a long train and was worn with a
veil of delicate hand-made lace. This bridal
ensemble includes numerous original
accessories such as "something blue" in
the form of a blue satin bow and garters
that feature delicate floral trim made of
ribbon work.

PLATE 100

Priscilla of Boston

Wedding Veil (above) and Wedding Dress (opposite), 1964 / Boston, Massachusetts / Silk, cotton, synthetic fabric /

Peabody Essex Museum

Priscilla of Boston, founded by Priscilla Kidder in 1945, is among the most acclaimed twentieth-century wedding gown design firms in America. The company attracted international attention for commissions such as the wedding gown worn by Tricia Nixon Cox to her wedding in the White House Rose Garden in 1971. This wedding gown, worn on July 19, 1964, by Phyllis Velis Houvouras at her marriage ceremony held at Boston's Greek Orthodox Cathedral, features a lace cape and train with hand-applied pearls and sequins, worn over the matching sleeveless dress.

PLATE 101

Wedding Dress, ca. 1845 / Southern United States / Cotton / Witte Museum

The hand-sewn wedding dress worn by Sarah Tate is a rare example of a wedding gown worn by an enslaved African-American woman who married during the antebellum period. Prior to the American Civil War, African-American slaves were denied the right to marry, a result of their master's legal right of ownership. Some slave owners allowed slaves to

marry informally but these relationships had no legal protection and could be severed by the master's command at any time.

Little is known about Sarah Tate's early life. Records indicate, however, that she was brought to Texas by the Edgar family of Concrete, DeWitt County, who possibly migrated from Tennessee. The style of the dress is characteristic of the 1840s and while fashionable, it is made of utilitarian cotton fabric. Sarah Tate, who lived to be almost 100 years of age,

saved this dress, her Bible, and a strand of beads that her mother brought from Africa throughout her long life.*

*Gladys-Marie Fry, *Stitched from the Soul: Slave Quilts from the Antebellum South* (Chapel Hill: University of North Carolina Press, 2002), 26–34; communication regarding accession records with Michaele Haynes, curator, Witte Museum, San Antonio, Texas, March 30, 2006.

PLATE 102

Christian Lacroix (b. 1951)
Wedding Cake Dress, late 1980s / Paris /
Silk / Collection of Sandy Schreier

Parisian couturier Christian Lacroix playfully
reinterprets the wedding cake in this fanciful
bridal gown from the late 1980s. Lacroix is
known for his use of luxurious fabrics, bold
shapes, and lavish hand-applied ornamentation such as the appliqués of rosettes and
swags on this dress. Lacroix concludes each
of his fashion runway shows with a bridal
ensemble as the ultimate expression of
fashionable dress.

WEDDING ATTIRE

Donald Clay Johnson

At their wedding, the bride and groom wear clothing that not only uniquely identifies them but also serves several other purposes. Numerous artistic expressions and flourishes in their dress and jewelry indicate cultural values, distinctive artistic expressions, and social or economic status. Their clothing may reflect older, more traditional approaches toward dress within a social group, or it may contain folklore injunctions—"something old, something new, something borrowed, something blue"—intended to ensure happiness for the bride and groom. Within some groups, especially those influenced by colonial

or yellow, an auspicious color associated with royalty, also prominently appears in Malay weddings.

The Japanese welcome elements from other cultures, adjust them to Japanese sensibilities, and incorporate them totally or partially into the Japanese way of life. In the post–World War II period, weddings in Japan have come to take place in secular facilities such as wedding halls or special wedding areas in hotels. Masami Suga noted that the present-day ceremony, which began to be observed about forty years ago, lasts about three hours, and consists of several components. The bride and groom change their attire for each of these segments, which provides the opportunity not only to wear several outfits but also to provide visual documentation between them. The component parts are the wedding proper, a reception, a memorial ceremony, and a departure ritual. Since there is no standard type of dress for each component, the couple may wear Japanese or Western clothing as they like. The wedding proper, typically a Shinto- or Christian-derived ceremony, begins the sequence of events. The bride and groom are dressed in traditional Japanese dress for a Shinto

PLATE 105 (above)
Umlak (bridegroom's wedding crown), 19th century / India / Repoussé silver with gilding / Los Angeles County Museum of Art

PLATE 106 (opposite)
Bridal Headdress, early 20th century / China / Silk, kingfisher feathers, metal, cotton, glass, other materials / Peabody Essex Museum

rite, or the bride wears a Western white wedding dress if observing Christian tradition. Upon the conclusion of the formal wedding the bride and groom change clothing for a reception that includes a series of speeches in their honor and the cutting of their wedding cake. The bride and groom then change clothing for a candle service during which memorial candles are lighted in honor of the couple's families followed by lighting a candle on each of the tables and greeting the guests seated at each table. A final change of clothes gets them into the clothing they wear to conclude the wedding.

Thus the white wedding gown often appears in Japanese weddings but in a uniquely Japanese way: It is but one of the numerous garments worn by the bride. This allows the Japanese to use the white wedding gown, as is so commonly done in many countries, but does not permit the white gown to dominate a Japanese wedding. The use of a Western white wedding gown in one of the wedding settings received encouragement in 1993 after the

wedding of the crown prince, when his bride, Masako Owada, a commoner, wore one as part of the ceremonies. Since only three commoners married into the royal family in the last millennium, Masako's dress attracted much attention among the Japanese public. Ceremonial dress of the Japanese royal family is quite archaic, however, and thus the style of the white dress worn in 1993 has not been adopted by contemporary Japanese brides, only the concept of having such a dress.

PLATE 107

Uchikake (outer robe), Edo period, 19th century / Japan / Satin damask (*rinzu*) with resist dyeing and silk / Museum of Fine Arts, Boston

PLATE 108

Uchikake (outer robe), Edo period, 19th century / Japan / Satin damask (*rinzu*) with resist dyeing and silk / Museum of Fine Arts, Boston

For a Shinto wedding, the bride wears an elaborate white kimono with distinctively Japanese artistic expressions. Whether a Shinto or a Christian ceremony, therefore, the bride wears white for the first component of her wedding. The symbolism of white is not the same between the two traditions, however. Whereas in the Western tradition white stands for purity, in the Shinto tradition it has two meanings. First, it is the color of death, and in the wedding conveys the notion of the bride "dying" to her family, while it also marks the transition to her new family. Second, white in the Shinto tradition represents birth, which in weddings means the bride is reborn into her husband's family. In earlier times, when Japanese weddings lasted three days, the bride wore white for two days before the final day when she wore a colorful kimono to signify her new life.

Wedding companies manage these interlocking events with their multiple changes of clothing within a Japanese wedding. Although the bride wears elaborate kimonos and gowns worth thousands of dollars, she actually rents them from the company. The wedding company takes care of all arrangements for the wedding, including dressing the bride. The bride comes to the wedding hall dressing area in simple clothing without makeup. Responsibility for dress changes for the bride presents the rental company with particular challenges. The complex Japanese kimono develops from folding, pinning, tucking, tying, and wrapping numerous layers of fabric, and the aesthetics of the bride's face requires special make-up and hair style (often partially resolved by the use of wigs). The transition to Western dress mandates much attention to make-up and hairstyle. This rental of bridal clothing for a Japanese wedding departs significantly from the attitude toward wedding clothing in most other societies. In the West and in Japan the groom's clothing is rented, but in most societies the bride or her family makes or purchases her dress, even though she wears it only once in her life.

Wedding attire, or aspects of it, often extends beyond the community of the bride or groom and is integrated into the ceremonies of diverse groups. The wide acceptance of the Western white wedding dress, for instance, transcends religion since Catholic, Protestant, and Jewish brides all freely wear it. In the Indian state of Gujarat, which has a religiously diverse society composed of Muslims, Hindus, and Jains, each group has its own unique sartorial customs, but they all use a common textile technique—tie and dye *(bandhani)*—to identify wedding clothing. They thus appear to desire a commonality in weddings based on production technique rather than item of fashion.

Plate 109 shows a tie-dye *odhni* (or *odhani*, a head shawl), the most prominent wedding garment of the Khatri Muslim community of Gujarat. The

PLATE 109 (top)
Odhani (woman's wedding headcover), late 19th–early 20th century / Kutch, Gujarat, India / Silk satin with tie-dye (*bandhani*) and metallic-thread embroidery / Los Angeles County Museum of Art

FIGURE 21 (right)
Odhani (woman's wedding headcover), ca. 1940 / India / Silk with tie-dye and badla technique, metallic-thread embroidery / Courtesy of Donald Clay Johnson

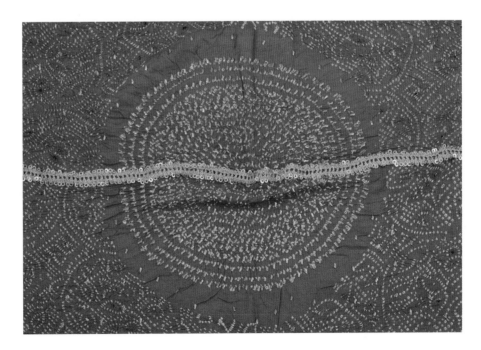

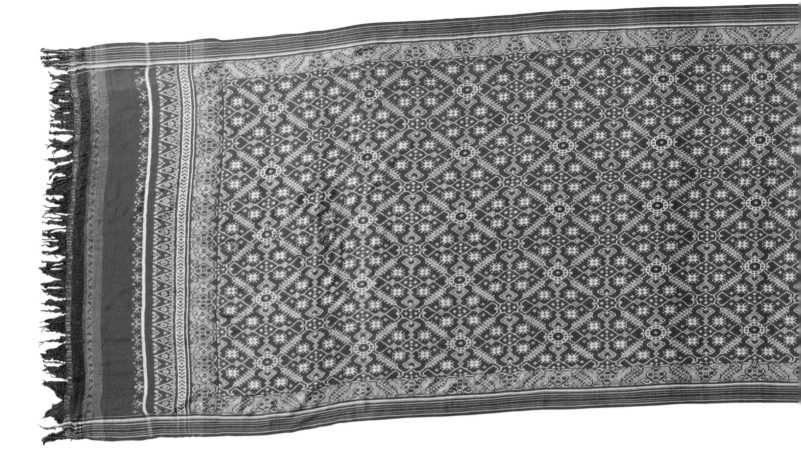

Khatri are one of the most famous Gujarati groups who produce fine tie-dye work and those used in their weddings are especially finely done. Enhancing its artistic tie-dye expression is the silver attached to the cloth either by using the *badla* technique, in which flattened metal is inserted into the cloth, or by embroidery. Plate 110 shows an odhni of another Muslim community in Gujarat. Its dominant yellow and red colors, however, strongly contrast with the red and black used by the Khatris. The band of black velvet with gold embroidery drapes over the bride's face and provides a rich accent to her and the jewelry she wears. Also distinctly different is the use of gold in the badla work rather than the silver used by the Khatris. Gold and silver not only make the cloth more costly, but Gujaratis consider both metals to be auspicious. The use of the precious metals as enhancements of the artistic design shows a commonality of approach among the religious communities, but the technique used varies among the Gujarati groups.

Although the Khatri's dominant black with a contrasting use of red reflects a distinctive color preference of this Muslim community, other Muslim groups favor red and yellow in their wedding colors, and the same colors are typically used by the Hindu and Jain communities of Gujarat. Red, a color symbolizing joy, appears in the tie-dye wedding garments of all the Gujarati

PLATE 110 (top)
Woman's Wedding Sari, 19th century / Patan, Gujarat, India / Silk plain weave with warp- and weft-resist dye (*patola*) and gold metallic thread supplementary weft / Los Angeles County Museum of Art

PLATE 111 (opposite)
Carolina Josephina von Franquemont (1817–1867)
Woman's Hip Wrapper, ca. 1850 / Semarang, Java, Indonesia / Cotton plain weave with hand-drawn wax resist (*batik tulis*) and applied gold (*prada*) / Los Angeles County Museum of Art

PLATE 112 (opposite)

Wedding Garments for Bride and Groom, 2004 / Imphal, Manipur, India / Groom's cotton pumyat with buttons (*kurta*): cotton, seeds, fabric. Bride's wedding dress (*potloi*): fabric, gold, silk, cotton, seeds / The Newark Museum

Located in northeast India, Manipur is noted for the distinctive style of wedding garments worn by the bride and groom. The bride's costume, called the *potloi*, features a skirt stiffened with canvas and cane and decorated with brass ornaments. The design of the jewelry is based on elements of the natural world including plants and seeds. The multilayered ensemble is sewn onto the bride prior to the wedding. A similar form of dress is worn for the *Rosa-lila*, the classical Manipuri ritual dance celebrating the Hindu love story of the deity Krishna and Radha, his consort and favorite among the *gopis*, cow-herding girls. The ensembles shown were specially created to record historic traditions and techniques used in Manipuri wedding dress, and have never been worn.

FIGURE 22 (above)

Wedding Sari, ca. 1940 / India / Cotton tie dyed and gold brocade / Courtesy of Donald Clay Johnson

communities. In the Hindu and Jain communities, a modest use of green tie-dye always appears as well. Green, which results from blending blue and yellow, serves to represent the blending of the two families through the wedding. Blue is also the color associated with the Hindu deity Krishna, while yellow relates to Radha, his consort, further strengthening the importance of incorporating green in wedding dress. In fact, the tie-dye process is symbolic in itself, as its production through closely binding the fabric speaks to the uniting of two families through marriage.

The *gharcholu* wedding saris Hindu and Jain brides receive from their mothers-in-law as part of the wedding ceremony (shown in figure 22) demonstrate a very different approach to tie-dye work. The grid pattern produced by gold thread woven into the fabric (*jari/zari*) defines squares that are filled with tie-dye art. The designs used in Gujarati tie-dye work, however, reflect the separate religious traditions. In observance of the Islamic proscription against portraying living things, Muslim designs are geometric. Designs on Jain fabrics focus upon flowers, while those of the Hindus display an exuberant use of flowers, animals, and dancing women.

Production of tie-dye fabrics varies significantly from that of other textile techniques since it is done as piecework in homes, where women do it along with their other household responsibilities. Such piecework provides an opportunity to earn additional funds for their families.

Fear of—and implied protection from—evil, especially the evil eye, and malicious spirits greatly affects what people wear at weddings. A Russian bride, for instance, wears gloves, which prevent her from ever directly touching anyone, thus avoiding contracting evil influences.

In coping with the potential malicious effects of spirits and the evil eye, the Berber people of North Africa have incorporated unique artistic expressions

STRAIGHTENING UP

THE MARRIAGE OF CONFORMITY AND

RESISTANCE IN WEDDING ART

Chrys Ingraham

One is not born a bride. Culture installs meaning in our lives from the very first moment we enter the social world. Everything from how we sit, stand, and feel to how we learn to interact according to our sex, class, or ethnic background, to how we practice heterosexuality is the product of the dominant culture and its social order. Frequently, the circulation of meanings we create is so significant, pervasive, and taken for granted that cultural constructions appear to occur naturally. In other words, we no longer see them as part of a social

landscape that we help to create. There are many cultural sites
through which this process is
visible but few as fertile as the
wedding and various representations of weddings for understanding how our social world
is organized, given meaning, and
implemented. As the entry point
for the institution of marriage,

PLATE 119
Julia Jacquette (b. 1964)
*White on White (Four Sections of Wedding
Dress) III*, 1997 / United States / Enamel on
wood panel / Courtesy of the artist

the wedding—particularly the white wedding—constitutes an exceptionally
rich spectacle for visual and performance artists. Considered historically, these
works have engaged with weddings and wedding artifacts, providing an ongoing and in-depth view of the cultural values and social priorities traditionally
associated with the experience of heterosexuality. While these works express a
host of themes, among the most compelling are those that reveal the disquiet-
ing marriage of conformity and resistance.

In Western societies today, the *white* wedding prevails as the dominant
form for this popular ritual, and is rapidly becoming the standard for weddings internationally. Although considered traditional, this type of wedding
is anything but. The stereotypical, lavish white wedding that has become a
highly prescribed spectacle featuring a bride in a formal white wedding gown,
a formally dressed groom, some combination of attendants and witnesses,
a religious ceremony, and an elaborate—and expensive—wedding reception
is largely the product of a host of very successful marketing campaigns. The
white wedding has become so overdetermined in the popular imagination that
to consider an alternative seems unthinkable.

As we enter the twenty-first century, with the ever-present realities of
globalization influencing social and cultural practices around the world, the
context for and images of weddings are changing dramatically. The white wedding is rapidly becoming an accepted and sought-after model for many non-
Western societies. Largely as a result of the growth and reach of the Internet,

PLATE 120
Julia Jacquette (b. 1964)
Four Wedding Veils, 1996 / United States /
Enamel on wood panel / Courtesy of the
artist

satellite communications, and mass media, the globalization of the white wedding mirrors the excesses of a globalized commodity culture that simultaneously contains and exploits difference and appears to leave little room for creativity. The mass-produced, mass-consumed, and extraordinarily expensive white wedding is both iconic and a cookie-cutter model for the average wedding. Approaching "McBride" status, the current white wedding functions as mass production and sacred ritual, defying reinterpretation, resistance, and creativity. As a cultural sacred the white wedding can be experienced by some as oppressive, making it a significant seedbed for artists whose passion and imagination is aroused by resistance to conformity.

Referred to by Wall Street analysts as "recession-proof," the wedding industry has reached such proportions that it can more accurately be described as a wedding-industrial complex. This structure reflects the close association among weddings, the transnational wedding industry, labor, global economics, marriage, the state, finance, religion, media, the Internet, and popular culture. Current Western industry estimates of the total annual revenues of the primary (white) wedding market are upwards of \$125 billion. Considered in relation to earnings, the cost of the average wedding in the United States represents 62.3 percent of the median earnings for a white family and 92 percent for black and Hispanic families. In Japan, with markets rivaling or exceeding American consumption patterns, couples are spending twice as much as Americans to create a two-ceremony wedding: a Western white wedding complete with Anglo clergy officiating followed by a traditional Japanese wedding. In Kenya, India, Mexico, and other parts of the world, brides are opting for a Western white wedding gown to supplement or actually replace the attire called for by their traditional ceremonies.[1]

PLATE 121

Claes Oldenburg (b. 1929)

Wedding Souvenir, 1966 / United States /

Plaster of Paris / Albright-Knox Art Gallery

The works chosen for this essay follow in the long-standing tradition of activist art by interrupting the taken-for-granted and contradictory landscape of weddings. Throughout history, people have used art and creativity to effect change and to find ways to address struggles. Whether in the context of mass efforts against repressive states or in the interest of effecting lesser forms of social change, art tells stories by intervening in the expected and shapes the way we think about issues. Activist wedding art challenges the production of white weddings as spectacles of accumulation and conformity and creates openings that allow us to imagine alternatives. Ultimately, these artists invite us to use the lens of wedding art to examine our social, economic, and cultural priorities and challenge our position as disinterested observer. They offer a global, historical, ideological, and sometimes humorous context and address the ways in which weddings have served as a symbolic target and site for social commentary in the United States and around the world.[2]

The title of this book—*Wedded Bliss*—itself offers commentary on the marriage of art and ceremony. When linked to weddings, bliss—a state of extreme happiness—can conjure up a fantasy of perfection and romance for many while provoking a cynical snicker from others. But a closer look at wedding art reveals a more complex relationship between weddings and marriage. Instead of finding a homogeneous representation of the wedding ritual, we discover a complex and contradictory landscape that reveals an important and consequential relationship: the marriage of conformity—the prescribed, the obligatory, the essential, the cultural sacred—and resistance.

Two works that make visible the homogeneity of weddings are Julia Jacquette's *White on White* paintings (1996–97; plates 119 and 120) and Sandy Skoglund's *The Wedding* (1994; plate 2).

In each instance, the artist's image conveys a homogeneous landscape as well as meaning system that is exceptionally complex. Within the prescription for the white wedding lies the possibility for change that contradiction enables. Jacquette uses repetition in a masterful way to signal a compliant practice, yet a close examination of her repetitive images reveals a host of intricacies in each plate. The challenge she presents is to the common-sense assumption that the white wedding conforms to tradition while a closer look reveals that the wedding objects are highly variant. The real contradiction she reveals is the notion that our wedding choices are somehow unique. At the same time the uniqueness is in the details not in the broad strokes. One walks away from her paintings ambivalent—feeling somewhat uncomfortable that the sameness was revealed and intrigued and captivated by the complexity of difference.

FIGURE 23
Florine Stettheimer (1871–1944)
The Cathedrals of Fifth Avenue, 1931 /
New York / Oil on canvas / Metropolitan
Museum of Art

Skoglund's red-on-red image is both defiant and obedient. The red breaks all the rules for color and purity, conveying a powerfully passionate image that is also complicated in its photograph of a couple challenged by the landscape they must negotiate. The conformist wedding participates in the illusion that the betrothed are new to each other and without lust or passion. Skoglund boldly interrupts this notion with the truth that the couple will *know* each other out loud—defying the codes that require their participation in a heterosexual order that requires some degree of reserve and chastity. The perspective in the photograph with the groom seeming larger than the bride and the bride appearing smaller, almost cowering and cornered, provides yet another commentary—that of predatory male to trapped female in a landscape that is both confining and laden with obstacles. This photograph projects a sense of outrage and discomfort; a feeling that defies the notion of well-being upon which depends the dominant meaning system about weddings.[3]

In Florine Stettheimer's canvas *Cathedrals of Fifth Avenue* (1931; figure 23), we find a surprisingly current commentary on the marriage of romance and materialism. Given the unprecedented level of consumerism in contemporary culture, this earlier critique reflects and anticipates what is to come as the wedding industry evolves.

At first glance, the viewer's eye is drawn to the white wedding taking place in the center of the painting. The still-veiled bride in her white wedding gown and the groom in his requisite tuxedo appear to be emerging from the canopy following their wedding. Contrary to the usual image of the unveiled bride and the newly wedded couple being celebrated by friends and family, this blessed couple is surrounded with images of chaos and consumerism. Stettheimer's veiled bride remains cloaked in illusion and fantasy, unaware of the culture she has enabled. With the name *Tiffany's* written across the sky, a Rolls Royce with a dollar sign on its grille, a Tarré couture shop, a billboard in production, photographers, vendors, and a parade complete with U.S. and City of New York flags, Stettheimer offers a somewhat heavy-handed depiction of the real celebrants of this wedding—the producers of capital and the state. To complete this image, Stettheimer includes a bishop offering a blessing next to someone in peasant clothing, who looks strikingly like Diego Rivera, the leftist artist, also offering a blessing. This comparison uses the Rivera figure to signify a materialist commentary that implicates the church in the production of capitalist exploitation. The entire landscape appears to offer a critique of weddings as overproduced spectacles of accumulation wrapped up in the interests of class struggle.

Stettheimer's *Cathedrals of Fifth Avenue* is charged with social commentary but it also pokes fun at the family, friends, dog, and spectators, all of whom are seemingly engaged with this event. Images of family appear both iconic and cartoonlike portraying the parents as statuesque and elite and the wed-

PLATE 122
Arthur Tress (b. 1940)
Untitled (Bride and Groom), 1970 / New York / Gelatin silver print / Smithsonian American Art Museum

PLATE 123

Teddy McMahon Pruett (b. 1948)

Fractured Wedding Ring: Divorce Attorney's Quilt, 2005 / United States / Recycled vintage textiles, aprons, crying towels, kitchen curtains, needlework, handkerchiefs, new and vintage cloth / Teddy McMahon Pruett

ding party as stiff and formal. Meanwhile images of children and other family members are depicted as comical and distracted.[4]

Arthur Tress's *Untitled (Bride and Groom)* [*Stephan Brecht, Bride and Groom*] (1970; plate 122) also provides a dramatic critique. In this photograph from his *Theater of the Mind* collection, Tress offers a social commentary on gender, marriage, and weddings using an actor and staged photography to show how enigmatic and contradictory our relationship to the social world is. Tress creates a setting that suggests the aftermath of destruction into which he places among the debris an individual who is both male and female, bride and groom. This incongruous image is contradicted by the oath-taking raised hand and stand-at-attention posture, implying some form of social compliance in the midst of obvious cultural and individual dissonance. The overall image is one of both confusion and coherence. The actor is at once different and the same, externally and internally one. Once again, we are greeted with the marriage of conformity and resistance.

Fractured Wedding Ring: Divorce Attorney's Quilt (2005; plate 123) by Teddy Pruett is an extraordinary example of weddings reinterpreted as art. Using the traditional "wedding ring" quilt as her model Pruett creates a commentary on the contemporary state of matrimony in American culture.

In the center of this his-and-hers quilt she stitched images of white, heterosexual couples imbued with romance and love along with the classic intertwined wedding ring which reads "With this ring I thee wed . . . until I change my mind." On the "her" side of the quilt Pruett provides a collage for the crying wife, who is now disillusioned with her marriage and her husband's failure to fulfill promises to love, honor, and cherish her. And on the "his" side the artist provides a medium for the husband to complain about how he can't make enough money to satisfy his wife, has to tolerate her mother, and has to endure her efforts to ruin his fun—cards, fishing, infidelity, and television. Among the most prominent images in this quilt is the large red heart that frames the marital conflict. The tension Pruett creates by overlaying this conflict with a signifier of love and romance sets up a dramatic commentary on the unmet expectations of the wedding promise. According to this template, expectations that make women economically dependent on and subservient to a man's need for power and play are central to this betrayal. All sewn up in this presentation of the traditional wedding-ring quilt is the gender system that undermines the promise of wedded bliss.

In her *Dada Poem Wedding Dress* (1994; plate 124), Lesley Dill presents another resistant wedding image in the form of a Victorian-style, corseted, paper wedding gown complete with tight bodice, train, and loose threads hanging from the hem and sleeves. Dill's enigmatic paper dress, defiant against the image of the perfect bride, presents instead a bride who is confined, soiled, and unraveling at the seams. Made for a Dada Ball AIDS benefit in New York, this virginal wedding dress was intended to serve as a reminder of the significant number of women who contracted HIV and with it lost their innocence. The copy of a biological heart contrasting against the text of Emily Dickinson's poem "The Soul has Bandaged Moments" with the phrase "moments of escape" imprinted across the waist of this tight-fitting gown delivers a cutting commentary on women's place in relation to marriage and domestic violence.

The dress was used for performance art during this benefit. As the words to Dickinson's poem were read, portions of the dress were torn apart word by word, signifying the tearing of the fabric of heterosexual illusion. At the end of this performance, the bride's naked body was painted with the same words of the poem. "With silent dignity she pulled a red ribbon from her mouth, mutely testifying to the survival and strength of the spirit."[5]

Similar to Tress's existential notion of duality, Dill inscribes Dickinson's inner contradictions into the very material of the bridal experience. This poem describes a woman who is at once bandaged and undone, "too appalled to stir," she "feels some ghastly Fright come up." She touches freedom and then "with shackles on the plumed feet" is recaptured by time and tradition, imprisoned by culture and history. Dill's dress offers an image of the antibride, devoid of any hint of perfection and confronted with structures that will ultimately break her spirit and destroy her.

The catharsis for Dill's bridal oppression could be E.V. Day's *Bride Fight* (2005; plate 125), in which veils, gloves, and gowns explode and transform any remnant of tradition and perfection. Each dress portrays a view of a conventional bride in a dramatic stop-action explosion. This textile-and-wire installation is constructed to represent a powerful explosion that blows the dresses up and off making room for the emergence of something unimagined. Day's "fight" seems light at first glance, but reveals a powerful discharge of emotions and confinement that Dickinson would have celebrated.[6]

PLATE 125

E. V. Day (b. 1967)

Bride Fight Installation, 2005 / United States / Polyester textile and accessories, fishing tackle, monofilament, paper, glue, wood, and metal / Courtesy of the artist and Deitch Projects

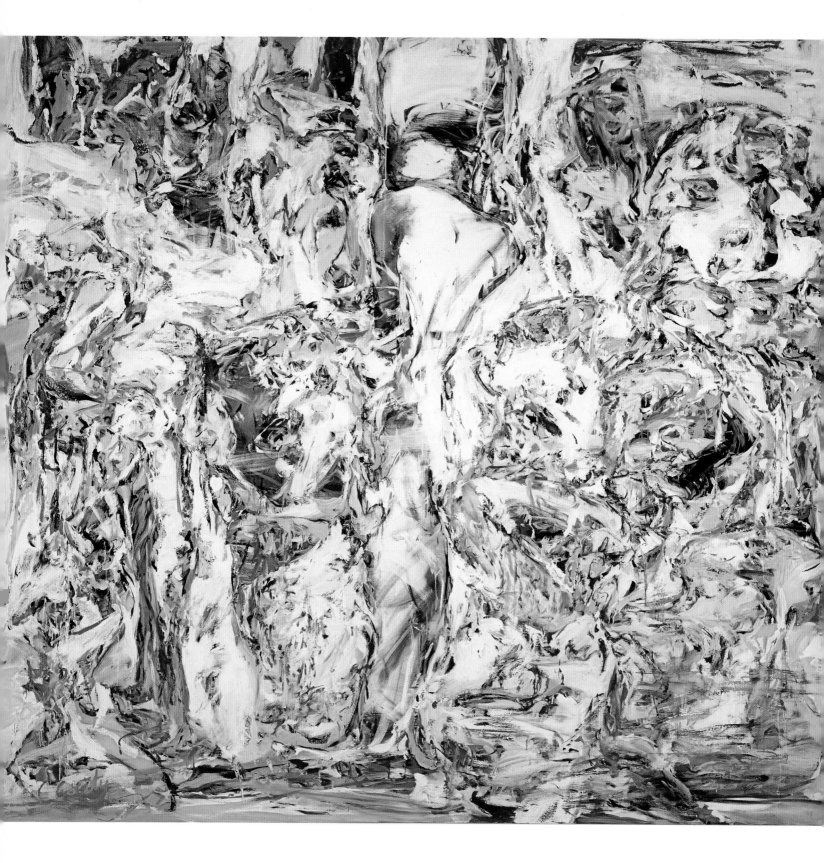

The other side of the confinement that Dill addresses is the experience of the family. Cecily Brown's canvas *Father of the Bride* (1999; plate 126), takes its title from the 1950s classic film of the same title, which was remade in 1991. The central theme in both films is the loss of the father's "little girl," which is played out against a backdrop of wedding-preparation chaos. The first impression Brown's work evokes is the image one might achieve by squinting at the chaos created by the mixing of white bodies and fabrics during the preparation for a white wedding. This work

PLATE 126

Cecily Brown (b. 1969)
Father of the Bride, 1999 / New York / Oil on canvas / Albright-Knox Art Gallery

FIGURE 24
Frida Kahlo (1907–1954)
My Grandparents, My Parents, and I (Family Tree), 1936 / Mexico / Oil and tempera on metal panel / Museum of Modern Art, New York

FIGURE 25
Gay Block (b. 1942) and Malka Drucker (b. 1945)
A Recontextualized Ketubbah, 1994 / United States / Chromogenic color print / The Jewish Museum, New York

appears to be less about social commentary than about the affective experience of the bride's father.

Another depiction of familial experience with weddings is found in Frida Kahlo's painting from 1936, *My Grandparents, My Parents, and I (Family Tree)* (figure 24). Using the format of the family tree, Kahlo offers a disturbing narrative on her birth, family, and history. She portrays herself as a very young child standing naked in the garden of her family home. Holding a red ribbon signifying an umbilical cord with one end leading to her maternal grandparents and the other to her paternal grandparents, Kahlo paints herself as a fetus in her mother's womb at the time of her parents' wedding. Defying cultural conventions of her time, Kahlo reveals the moment of conception and unveils the truth about her birth and her parents' premarital sexuality. To accomplish this, she portrays her parents and grandparents as compliant subjects following the social order of their time, with her mother standing in the obligatory position and posture of the good wife. While Kahlo was frequently fascinated with her origins, this painting goes beyond origins to the place of moral hypocrisy in the social world.

As we consider the relationship of conformity and resistance in the marriage of art and ceremony, it is also important to observe the way in which works of art allow us to imagine alternatives. *New Jerusalem* by Sister Gertude Morgan (1960; plate 127), represents a primitive but significant effort to depict her religious evangelism. Drawn from the New Testament book of Revelation, Sister Gertude's vision of a New Jerusalem is of a land where Jesus is of African descent, the skies are filled with multicultural angels, and Sister Gertrude herself is the bride of Christ.[7]

PLATE 127

Sister Gertrude Morgan (1900–1980)
New Jerusalem, ca. 1960 / New Orleans,
Louisiana / Acrylic and ink on cardboard /
Louisiana State Museum

Similarly, Gay Block and Malka Drucker's piece, *A Recontextualized Ketub-bah* (1994; figure 25), shows us their Jewish marriage contract, which frames the couple's wedding portrait, offering an alternative image in the form of a lesbian wedding. Along with the Sister Gertrude Morgan, Block and Drucker reframe the marriage of art and ceremony as inclusive and varied, establishing a wedding landscape that reclaims tradition in the name of "other."

Finally, Robert Boyd's *Cake Cutter* (plate 118), *True Blue*, and *L'Age d'Or* (figure 26), from his 2001 show "The Virgin Collection," calls an end to our romance with the white wedding by offering a variety of images that shatter associations of weddings with innocence and purity. When Boyd was in Seville, Spain, he was struck by the number of bridal shops and reminded by the wedding attire of its similar-

ity to the white-hooded robes worn by Jewish "heretics" during the Spanish Inquisition as well as those worn by the white supremacist Ku Klux Klan in the United States. Boyd creates a show of wedding art that intervenes commonplace notions of the white wedding. By "cutting" through the ideology of romance associated with this dominant form, Boyd offers an analysis of heterosexuality as imbricated in both racism and heterosexism, and he changes the viewer's idealized notion of weddings forever.[8]

Considered together, all of these works dismantle and challenge the taken-for-granted and offer an alternative perspective to the romanticized experience of weddings and marriage. These reinterpretations tell a story the wedding-industrial complex would prefer to suppress. It is a tale of confining, oppressive, contradictory, and silenced lives. These works convey a message about gender, sexuality, and race that historically has been embedded in traditions that uphold forms of dominance while obliterating real needs and the freedom to be who we are. They reveal the ways in which our romance with weddings and tradition manages the contradictions and disillusions that come with scripts and cultural mandates. To be without choice, without the variability that is central to all life, is to live outside of bliss. It is to die to life itself.

ENDNOTES

1   Chrys Ingraham, *White Weddings: Romancing Heterosexuality in Popular Culture,* 2d ed. (New York: Routledge, 2008).

2   Deborah Barndt, ed., *Wild Fire: Art as Activism* (Toronto: Sumach Press, 2006).

3   Charles Hagen, "The Wedding by Sandy Skoglund," *New York Times* (September 23, 1994): C1.

4   Florine Stettheimer, *The Cathedrals of Fifth Avenue* (New York: Metropolitan Museum of Art, 1931). www.metmuseum.org/explore/artists_view/cathedrals_tide.html

5   Nina Felshin, "Women's Work: A Lineage, 1966–94," *Art Journal* (Spring 1995): 71–85.

6   E. V. Day, *Bride Fight* (New York: Deitch Projects, 2006). www.deitch.com

7   William A. Fagley, Jason Berry, and Helen Shannon, *Tools of Her Ministry: The Art of Sister Gertrude Morgan* (New York: American Folk Museum and Rizzoli, 2004).

8   Holland Cotter, "Robert Boyd—'The Virgin Collection'," *New York Times* (November 22, 2002): C1.

EXHIBITION CHECKLIST

This checklist provides information about artwork included in the exhibition. The plates in this publication represent artwork in the exhibition; the works featured as figure illustrations are not included in the exhibition. The works in this checklist are arranged alphabetically by artist's name; works by unidentified artists follow and are listed alphabetically by descriptive title. Plate numbers are indicated in **bold type** and enclosed in square brackets following the title and date of the work. Dimensions are provided in inches and in metric equivalents; height precedes width precedes depth, and any exceptions are noted. Figure information is listed at the conclusion of the checklist.

Mary Kawennatakie Adams (1917–1999)
Wedding Cake Basket, 1986 **[8]**
Kahnawake Mohawk Nation, St. Regis, Quebec
Woven ash splint and sweet grass
25 1/2 x 15 3/4 inches (64.8 x 40 cm)
Smithsonian American Art Museum, gift of Herbert Waide Hemphill, Jr., 1989.30.1A–E

Tiziana and Gianni Baldizzone
Berber Wedding, 2000 **[80]**
Morocco
Pigment print on photographic paper
20 x 30 inches (50.8 x 76.2 cm)
Tiziana and Gianni Baldizzone

Tiziana and Gianni Baldizzone
Black Miao Wedding, 2000 **[85]**
South Eastern Guizhou, China
Pigment print on photographic paper
20 x 30 inches (50.8 x 76.2 cm)
Tiziana and Gianni Baldizzone

Tiziana and Gianni Baldizzone
Fassi Wedding, 2000 **[84]**
Fez, Morocco
Pigment print on photographic paper
20 x 30 inches (50.8 x 76.2 cm)
Tiziana and Gianni Baldizzone

Tiziana and Gianni Baldizzone
Kazakh Couple in Their Yurt, 2005 **[86]**
Mount Altai, Xinjiang Province, China
Pigment print on photographic paper
20 x 30 inches (50.8 x 76.2 cm)
Tiziana and Gianni Baldizzone

Tiziana and Gianni Baldizzone
Minangkabau Bride and Groom, 2001 **[79]**
West Sumatra, Indonesia

Pigment print on photographic paper
20 x 30 inches (50.8 x 76.2 cm)
Tiziana and Gianni Baldizzone

Tiziana and Gianni Baldizzone
Tamil Wedding, 2000 **[82]**
Chennai, India
Pigment print on photographic paper
20 x 30 inches (50.8 x 76.2 cm)
Tiziana and Gianni Baldizzone

Tiziana and Gianni Baldizzone
Tibetan Nomad Bride, 1991 **[81]**
Qinghai Province, China
Pigment print on photographic paper
20 x 30 inches (50.8 x 76.2 cm)
Tiziana and Gianni Baldizzone

Tiziana and Gianni Baldizzone
Wodaabee Wedding, 1999 **[83]**
Niger
Pigment print on photographic paper
20 x 30 inches (50.8 x 76.2 cm)
Tiziana and Gianni Baldizzone

Bikash Bhattacharjee (1940–2006)
Thakur Mathura Das, 1982 **[42]**
India
Oil on canvas
36 x 35 3/4 inches (91.4 x 90.8 cm)
Peabody Essex Museum, Chester and David Herwitz Collection, 2000, E301035

Designed by Karl Bitter (1867–1915)
Manufactured by William B. Durgin Company
Standing Cup, ca. 1900 **[60]**
Concord, New Hampshire
Gold
14 3/8 x 5 1/16 inches (dia.) (36.5 x 12.9 cm);
Weight: 2,559.60 grams
The Metropolitan Museum of Art, Gift of Marcus I. Goldman, 1948, 48.173

Robert Boyd (b. 1969)
Cake Cutter, 2002 **[118]**
New York
Digital Duraflex print
24 x 20 inches (61 x 50.8 cm)
Jeremy E. Steinke Collection, New York

Cecily Brown (b. 1969)
Father of the Bride, 1999 **[126]**
New York
Oil on canvas
100 x 110 inches (254 x 279.4 cm)
Albright-Knox Art Gallery, Buffalo, NY, Sarah Norton Goodyear Fund, 1999, 1999.17

Cile Bellefleur Burbidge (b. 1926)
Architectural Fantasy Cake, 2007 **[6]**
Danvers, Massachusetts
Royal icing
36 x 27 x 27 inches (91.4 x 68.6 x 68.6 cm)
Courtesy of the artist

Marc Chagall (1887–1985)
Bride with Fan, 1911 **[87]**
Paris
Oil on canvas
Unframed: 18 x 15 inches (45.7 x 38.1 cm)
Framed: 27 1/2 x 24 1/4 x 2 inches (69.9 x 61.2 x 5.1 cm)
The Metropolitan Museum of Art, The Pierre and Maria-Gaetana Matisse Collection, 2002, 2002.456.8

James Wells Champney (1843–1903)
Wedding Presents, ca. 1880 **[9]**
United States
Oil on canvas
41 x 48 inches (104.1 x 121.9 cm)
Museum of the City of New York, gift of Mr. & Mrs. Luke Vincent Lockwood, 42.254

John Clevely, Sr. (1712–1777)
The Landing of Her Majesty Queen Charlotte at the Port of Harwich, 1762 **[36]**
England
Oil on canvas
Unframed: 33 1/4 x 66 1/4 inches (84.5 x 168.3 cm)
Framed: 36 1/2 x 69 3/4 inches (92.7 x 177.2 cm)
Anonymous loan

John Collet (1725–1780), Artist
Jabez Goldar (1729–1795), Engraver
Modern Love, Plate I, Courtship, 1765 **[14]**
London, England
Colored line engraving
Framed: 17 1/4 x 21 inches (43.8 x 53.3 cm)
The Colonial Williamsburg Foundation, 1969-192,1

John Collet (1725–1780), Artist
Jabez Goldar (1729–1795), Engraver
Modern Love, Plate II, The Elopement, 1765 **[15]**
London, England
Colored line engraving
Framed: 17 1/4 x 21 inches (43.8 x 53.3 cm)
The Colonial Williamsburg Foundation, 1969-192,2

John Collet (1725–1780), Artist
Jabez Goldar (1729–1795), Engraver
Modern Love, Plate III, The Honeymoon, 1765 **[16]**
London, England
Colored line engraving

Framed: 17 1/4 x 21 inches (43.8 x 53.3 cm)
The Colonial Williamsburg Foundation, 1969-
192,3

John Collet (1725–1780), Artist
Jabez Goldar (1729–1795), Engraver
Modern Love, Plate IV, Discordant Matrimony,
1765 [17]
London, England
Colored line engraving
Framed: 17 1/4 x 21 inches (43.8 x 53.3 cm)
The Colonial Williamsburg Foundation, 1969-
192,4

Attributed to Nathaniel Currier (1813–1888)
The Seven Stages of Matrimony, 1845 [5]
New York
Lithograph
Image: 8 1/2 x 13 inches (21.6 x 33 cm)
Sheet: 13 x 17 3/4 inches (33 x 45.1 cm)
American Antiquarian Society, Worcester,
Massachusetts

E. V. Day (b. 1967)
Bride Fight Scale Model, 2006 [125]
United States
Polyester textile and accessories, fishing
tackle, monofilament, paper, glue, wood, and
metal
26 x 29 3/8 x 33 1/4 inches (66 x 74.6 x 84.5
cm)
Courtesy of the artist and Deitch Projects

Lesley Dill (b. 1950)
Dada Poem Wedding Dress, 1994 [124]
New York
Acrylic and thread on paper on mannequin
64 x 60 x 70 inches (162.6 x 152.4 x 177.8 cm)
Collection of the Orlando Museum of Art,
Acquisition Trust Purchase, 1996, 96.65

Painted by Victor Eeckhout (1821–1879); made
by J. Duvelleroy
Fan, "Moorish Wedding," ca. 1875 [72]
Paris
Skin leaf, painted in oils; carved ivory sticks
with gilt details; paste stone
H 11 1/4 x L 21 1/4 inches (28 x 54 cm)
Museum of Fine Arts, Boston, Oldham
Collection, 1976.271

Sarah Goodridge (1788–1853)
Beauty Revealed (Self-Portrait), 1828 [20]
Boston, Massachusetts
Watercolor on ivory
2 5/8 x 3 1/8 inches (6.7 x 7.9 cm)
The Metropolitan Museum of Art, gift of
Gloria Manney, 2006, 2006.235.74

Laura Coombs Hills (1859–1952)
The Bride, 1908 [1]
Newburyport, Massachusetts
Watercolor on ivory
5 1/8 x 3 1/8 inches (13.1 x 8 cm)
Museum of Fine Arts, Boston, gift of Laura
Coombs Hills, 51.1928

William Hogarth (1697–1764)
*The Wedding of Stephen Beckingham and Mary
Cox*, 1729 [13]
London, England
Oil on canvas
Unframed: 50 1/2 x 40 1/2 inches (128.3 x
102.9 cm)
Framed: 55 1/2 x 45 1/2 x 2 7/8 inches (141 x
115.6 x 5.2 cm)
The Metropolitan Museum of Art, Marquand
Fund, 1936, 36.111

Winslow Homer (1836–1910)
Rustic Courtship, 1874 [19]
New England
Watercolor and gouache on paper
8 3/4 x 12 5/8 inches (22.2 x 32.1 cm)
Collection of Mr. and Mrs. Paul Mellon,
Upperville, Virginia

Peggy Hoyt, Inc.
Wedding Gown and Accessories, 1931 [99]
New York
Silk and other materials
58 x 30 x 65 inches (147.3 x 76.2 x 165.1 cm)
Peabody Essex Museum, gift of Mr. Randolph
P. Barton, 2002, 138241

Julia Jacquette (b. 1964)
Four Wedding Veils, 1996 [120]
United States
Enamel on wood panel
21 x 21 inches (53.3 x 53.3 cm)
Courtesy of the artist

Julia Jacquette (b. 1964)
*White on White (Four Sections of Wedding
Dress) III*, 1997 [119]
United States
Enamel on wood panel
26 x 26 inches (66 x 66 cm)
Courtesy of the artist

William H. Johnson (1901–1970)
The Honeymooners, 1941–1944 [77]
New York
Oil on plywood
28 7/8 x 26 inches (73.3 x 66 cm)
Smithsonian American Art Museum, gift of
the Harmon Foundation, 1967.59.629

Attributed to C. Kahrs
Wedding Cup, 17th century [50]
Europe, possibly Bergen, Norway
Silver and silver gilt
8 x 3 1/8 inches (dia.) (20.3 x 7.9 cm)
The Sargent House Museum, Gloucester,
Massachusetts, #139

Alex Katz (b. 1927)
Wedding Dress, 1993 [3]
United States
Aquatint and etching
52 x 22 inches (132.1 x 55.9 cm)
Courtesy of Barbara Krakow Gallery

Ivar Kvalen
Painted Chest, 1777 [33]
Gubrandsdal, Norway
Painted wood, iron
33 x 69 1/4 x 28 3/8 inches (83.8 x 175.9 x 72.1 cm)
Minneapolis Institute of Arts, gift of Joel and
Irene Njus in memory of Siri Ivar's datter
Grosberg, 99.93a,b

Christian Lacroix (b. 1951)
Wedding Cake Dress, late 1980s [102]
Paris
Silk
60 x 34 (chest) x 24 (waist) x 35 1/2 (hips)
inches (152.4 x 86.4 x 61 x 90.2 cm)
Collection of Sandy Schreier

Jacob Lawrence (1917–2000)
The Wedding, 1948 [70]
United States
Egg tempera on hardboard
20 x 24 inches (50.8 x 61 cm)
The Art Institute of Chicago, restricted gift
of Mary P. Hines in memory of her mother,
Frances W. Pick, 1993.258

Maison Ruffie
Mariage de Mademoiselle Lucie Wheatland,
1921 [93]
Paris
Watercolor and gouache on paper
Closed: 16 x 12 1/2 inches (40.6 x 30.5 x 1.3 cm)
Peabody Essex Museum, gift of Mrs. John F.
Fulton, 1988, 137270

Gari Melchers (1860–1932)
The Wedding, ca. 1892 [71]
United States
Oil on canvas
Unframed: 43 x 26 inches (109.2 x 66 cm)
Framed: 52 3/8 x 35 x 3 inches (133 x 88.9 x
7.6 cm)
Albright-Knox Art Gallery, Charles W.
Goodyear Fund, 1999, 1922.7

Sister Gertrude Morgan (1900–1980)
New Jerusalem, c. 1960 **[127]**
New Orleans, Louisiana
Acrylic and ink on cardboard
11 1/2 x 14 inches (29.2 x 35.6 cm)
Louisiana State Museum, 1981.02

William Sidney Mount (1807–1868)
The Sportsman's Last Visit, 1835 **[18]**
New York
Oil on canvas
Unframed: 21 1/4 x 17 1/4 inches (54 x 43.8 cm)
Framed: 24 1/2 x 20 1/2 inches (62.2 x 52.1 cm)
The Long Island Museum of American Art, History & Carriages, gift of Mr. and Mrs. Ward Melville, 1958, 0.1.20

Claes Oldenburg (b. 1929)
Wedding Souvenir, 1966 **[121]**
United States
Plaster of Paris
5 7/8 x 2 1/4 x 6 5/8 inches (14.9 x 5.7 x 16.8 cm)
Albright-Knox Art Gallery, Buffalo, NY, gift of James Elliot, 1982, 1982.48.1

Sophia Amelia Peabody (1809–1871)
Villa Menaggio, Lago di Como [View of Lake Como, Italy], 1839–1840 **[25]**
Salem, Massachusetts
Oil on canvas
Framed: 13 1/2 x 16 1/2 inches (34.3 x 41.9 cm)
Peabody Essex Museum, gift of Joan D. Ensor, in memory of her mother, Imogen Hawthorne, granddaughter of Sophia and Nathaniel Hawthorne, 2004, 138520

Sophia Amelia Peabody (1809–1871)
Isola San Giovanni [View of Lake Como, Italy], 1839–1840 **[24]**
Salem, Massachusetts
Oil on canvas
Framed: 13 1/2 x 16 1/2 inches (34.3 x 41.9 cm)
Peabody Essex Museum, gift of Joan D. Ensor, in memory of her mother, Imogen Hawthorne, granddaughter of Sophia and Nathaniel Hawthorne, 2004, 138521

Pablo Picasso (1881–1973)
Jacqueline Dressed as a Bride, 1961 **[39]**
France
Aquatint and etching
Plate: 15 5/8 x 11 5/8 inches (39.7 x 29.5 cm)
Sheet: 20 1/4 x 16 inches (51.4 x 40.6 cm)
The Metropolitan Museum of Art, Purchase, Reba and Dave Williams Gift, 1997, 1997.90

Priscilla of Boston
Wedding gown and veil, 1964 **[100]**
Boston, Massachusetts
Silk, cotton, synthetic fabric
54 1/2 x 48 x 51 inches (with train) (138.4 x 121.9 x 129.5 cm)
Peabody Essex Museum, gift of Phyllis Velis Houvouras, 2003, 138587.1-3

Teddy McMahon Pruett (b. 1948)
Fractured Wedding Ring: Divorce Attorney's Quilt, 2005 **[123]**
United States
Recycled vintage textiles, aprons, crying towels, kitchen curtains, needlework, handkerchiefs, new and vintage cloth
72 x 59 inches (182.9 x 149.9 cm)
Courtesy of the artist

Augustus Saint-Gaudens (1848–1907)
Mrs. Stanford White (Bessie Springs Smith), 1893 **[40]**
Cornish, New Hampshire
Bronze
14 1/4 inches (dia.) (36.2 cm)
The Metropolitan Museum of Art, gift of Anne Tonetti Gugler, 1981, 1981.55.1

Maria Sanchez de la Cruz
Wedding Huipil, 20th century **[114]**
Zinacantan or Nachis, Chiapas, Mexico
Cotton, feathers
44 3/16 x 36 1/4 inches (112.2 x 92.1 cm)
Lent by the Minneapolis Institute of Arts, gift of Richard L. Simmons, 2000.136

Heikki Seppä (b. 1927)
Lupin Wedding Crown, 1982 **[11]**
United States
Gold, silver, diamond
8 inches (dia.) (20.3 cm)
Smithsonian American Art Museum, gift of the James Renwick Alliance, 2001.46

Srilekha Sikander (b. 1950)
The Fisherman's Wedding, 1997 **[76]**
India
Watercolor on paper
21 1/4 x 27 5/6 inches (54 x 70.7 cm)
Peabody Essex Museum, The Chester and David Herwitz Collection, 2000, E300985

Amrit and Rabindra Singh
Nyrmla's Wedding II, 1985–1986 **[41]**
England
Poster paint, gouache, and gold dust on mountboard
30 x 20 inches (76.2 x 50.8 cm)
Courtesy of the artist © The Singh Twins
artists: www.singhtwins.co.uk

Dayanita Singh (b. 1961)
Sistine Chapel, Calcutta 1999, 1999 **[47]**
India
Silver gelatin print on aluminum
39 3/8 x 39 3/8 inches (100 x 100 cm)
Courtesy of the artist and Frith Street Gallery, London, DS 9

Dayanita Singh (b. 1961)
Nagaur Fort, Delhi 2000, 2000 **[46]**
India
Silver gelatin print on aluminum
39 3/8 x 39 3/8 inches (100 x 100 cm)
Courtesy of the artist and Frith Street Gallery, London, DS 8

Sandy Skoglund (b. 1946)
The Wedding, 1994 **[2]**
United States
Silver dye bleach (Cibachrome)
Unframed: 38 5/8 x 48 1/2 inches (98.1 x 123.2 cm)
Framed: 44 x 53 7/8 inches (111.8 x 136.8 cm)
Columbus Museum of Art, Ohio; Museum Purchase, Howald Fund, 1994
©1994 Sandy Skoglund

Mara Superior (b. 1951)
A Swan's Wedding Day, 2007 **[7]**
Massachusetts
Ceramics and glass
20 x 12 x 7 inches (50.8 x 30.5 x 17.8 cm)
Courtesy of the artist and Ferrin Gallery

James Symonds (1633–1714)
Joseph and Bathsheba Pope Valuables Cabinet, 1679 **[32]**
Salem, Massachusetts
Oak, maple, iron, paint
16 1/2 x 17 x 9 1/2 inches (41.9 x 43.2 x 24.1 cm)
Peabody Essex Museum, museum purchase, 2000, 138011

Abbott Handerson Thayer (1849–1921)
A Bride, ca. 1895 **[38]**
New England
Oil on canvas
21 x 17 1/8 inches (53.3 x 43.5 cm)
Smithsonian American Art Museum, gift of John Gellatly, 1929.6.111

Tiffany & Co.
Anniversary Cup, 1891 **[59]**
New York
Silver gilt
8 7/8 x 7 3/8 inches (22.5 x 18.7 cm)
Anonymous loan, Courtesy of the Minneapolis Institute of Arts

Tiffany & Co.
Anniversary Napkin Rings and Box, ca. 1873
[55]
New York
Sterling silver, leather, paper, silk, wood, brass
Ring: 2 x 2 1/8 x 1 1/2 inches (5 x 5.5 x 4 cm)
Ring box: 3 1/8 x 5 7/8 x 3 7/8 inches (8 x 14.8 x 9.7 cm)
Tiffany & Co. Archives, B2006.16.01a-b

Tiffany & Co.
Anniversary Vase, 1900 [58]
New York
Wood and silver
11 1/2 x 5 1/8 x 4 1/4 inches (29 x 13 x 11 cm)
Tiffany & Co. Archives, B2005.03

Tiffany & Co.
"Dog Collar" Style Necklace with Box, 1904 [53]
New York
Gold, enamel, pearl, turquoise, diamonds
1 1/4 x 14 1/4 inches (3.2 x 36.2 cm)
Tiffany & Co. Archives, A1999.51.01(necklace) and .02 (box)

Tiffany & Co.
Golden Anniversary Puff Box, 1869 [56]
New York
Sterling silver, gold
3 1/2 x 5 1/8 inches (dia.) (9 x 13 cm)
Tiffany & Co. Archives, B2006.28

Tiffany & Co.
Tenth Anniversary Bracelet, 1865 [54]
New York
Gold, enamel, diamonds
2/3 x 2 1/2 x 2 1/4 inches (1.7 x 6.4 x 5.7 cm)
Bowdoin College Library, Joshua L. Chamberlain Collection, George J. Mitchell Department of Special Collections & Archives, M27.13

Ricky Tims (b. 1956)
Shekinah (chupah or wedding canopy), 1995 [45]
Texas
Quilted textiles
81 x 67 inches (205.7 x 170.2 cm)
Courtesy of Dr. Isaac and Isabel Boniuk

Arthur Tress (b. 1940)
Untitled (Bride and Groom), 1970 [122]
New York
Gelatin silver print
Image: 10 3/8 x 10 7/16 inches (26.4 x 26.5 cm)
Sheet: 14 x 11 inches (35.6 x 27.9 cm)
Smithsonian American Art Museum, Transfer from the National Endowment for the Arts, 1983.63.1490

James Van Der Zee (1886–1983)
Journey of Life, 1939
New York
Silver print
9 15/16 x 7 7/8 inches (25.2 x 20 cm)
The New Jersey State Museum, purchased with contributions from Louis and Rhonda Rosser, Edward Anderson, William and Jessica Granville, Lawrence Hilton, Bellevue Gallery, New Jersey Black Administrators' Network and Museum Purchase, FA1982.60

Carolina Josephina von Franquemont (1817–1867)
Woman's Hip Wrapper, ca. 1850 [111]
Semarang, Java, Indonesia
Cotton plain weave with hand-drawn wax resist (batik tulis) and applied gold (prada)
42 x 80 3/8 inches (106.7 x 204.3 cm)
Los Angeles County Museum of Art, Inger McCabe Elliott Collection, M.91.184.330

Benjamin West (1738–1820)
Self-Portrait, 1758 or 1759 [21]
Philadelphia
Watercolor on ivory
2 1/2 x 1 13/16 inches (6.4 x 4.6 cm)
Yale University Art Gallery, Lelia A. and John Hill Morgan, B.A. 1893, LL.B. 1896, M.A. (Hon.) 1929, Collection, 1940.529

Brian White (b. 1960)
Vintage White Dress and Veil, 2007 [43]
Union, Maine
Shell, metal, paint, epoxy
Dress: 65 x 36 inches (165.1 x 91.4 cm)
Veil: 48 x 28 11 inches (dia.) (121.9 x 71.1 x 27.9 cm)
Courtesy of the artist

Ebenezer White
Busk, 1782 [22]
Vermont
Carved wood
12 1/8 x 3 7/8 x 1/4 inches (30.8 x 9.8 x 0.5 cm)
Winterthur Museum & Country Estate, gift of John A. Gergen, Kenneth J. Gergen, Stephen L. Gergen and David R. Gergen, 92.87

Rachel Goodwin Woodnutt (1787–1828)
Quilt, 1827–1828 [57]
Salem, New Jersey
Silk, cotton
109 x 118 inches (276.9 x 299.7 cm)
Winterthur Museum & Country Estate, gift of Miss Elizabeth Newlin Baker, 1960.34.3

Advertising Art Photograph for Priscilla of Boston, 1954 [90]
Boston, Massachusetts
Gelatin silver print
Image: 14 x 11 1/4 inches (35.6 x 28.6 cm)
Mat: 14 5/8 x 12 inches (37.2 x 30.5 cm)
Peabody Essex Museum, gift of Priscilla C. Kidder, 2003, 138429.9

Advertising Art Photograph for Priscilla of Boston, 1955 [89]
Boston, Massachusetts
Gelatin silver print
Image: 14 x 11 1/4 inches (35.6 x 28.6 cm)
Mat: 16 1/2 x 13 inches (41.9 x 33 cm)
Peabody Essex Museum, gift of Priscilla C. Kidder, 2003, 138429.4

Advertising Art Photograph for Priscilla of Boston, ca. 1970 [88]
Boston, Massachusetts
Gelatin silver print
Image: 13 7/8 x 9 3/8 inches (35.2 x 23.8 cm)
Mat: 16 x 11 1/2 inches (40.6 x 29.2 cm)
Peabody Essex Museum, gift of Priscilla C. Kidder, 2003, 138429.23

After the Wedding in Warren, Pennsylvania, after 1916 or 1920 [78]
Pennsylvania
Oil on canvas
Unframed: 22 1/16 x 29 5/16 inches (56 x 74.5 cm)
Framed: 25 1/2 x 33 1/2 inches (64.8 x 85.1 cm)
National Gallery of Art, Washington, gift of Edgar William and Bernice Chrysler Garbisch, 1980.61.10

A-ndef (drum), early 20th century [51]
Baga peoples, Guinea
Wood, pigment, hide
44 1/2 x 12 1/4 x 14 1/2 inches (113 x 31.1 x 36.8 cm)
National Museum of African Art, Smithsonian Institution, Purchased with funds provided by the Smithsonian Collections Acquisition Program and gift of the Annie Laurie Aitken Charitable Trust, the Frances and Benjamin Benenson Foundation, David C. Driskell, 91-1-1

Anniversary Teapot, 1866 [52]
United States
Tinplate, painted cast pewter handle, and lead solder
9 1/2 x 10 x 4 1/8 inches (24.1 x 25.4 x 10.5 cm)
Abby Aldrich Rockefeller Folk Art Museum, The Colonial Williamsburg Foundation, Williamsburg, VA, 1989.808.1

The Annunciation, Carriage Cushion Cover, late 18th century [29]
Sweden
Tapestry woven wool and linen
18 1/2 x 38 1/5 inches (47 x 97 cm)
The Khalili Collection of Swedish Textile Art, Inv. no. sw.29

Bridal Headdress, 19th century [129]
China
Kingfisher feathers, silk, enamel, brass, beads, pearls, semiprecious stones
11 1/2 x 12 1/2 x 9 inches (29.21 x 31.75 x 22.86 cm)
Peabody Essex Museum, gift in honor of Mr. and Mrs. Austin Cheney by their daughters Ruth C. Krumhaat, Marjorie B.C. Shaw, Elizabeth C. Buckley, and Mabel C. Smith, 1984, E75225.A

Bridal Headdress, early 20th century [106]
China
Silk, kingfisher feathers, metal, cotton, glass, other materials
13 x 16 x 24 inches (33 x 40.6 x 61 cm)
Peabody Essex Museum, gift of Mr. and Mrs. Ward I. Gregg, 1979, E80986.A

Bridal Wreath Headpiece, 1859 [12]
Rowley, Massachusetts
Silk, wax, wire, cotton
2 1/2 x 9 1/2 x 10 inches (6.4 x 24.1 x 25.4 cm)
Peabody Essex Museum, gift of Mrs. Harry H. Gould, 1944, 125688

Brisé Fan, ca. 1810 [73]
Italy, possibly Russia
Silver filigree blades with silk ribbon
7 7/8 x 14 3/8 inches (20 x 36.5 cm)
Museum of Fine Arts, Boston, Oldham Collection, 1976.354

Bzayi (fibula), early 20th century [116]
Kabyle peoples, Kabylie, Algeria
Silver alloy, color, enamel
7 1/2 x 3 3/4 x 5/8 inches (19.1 x 9.6 x 1.6 cm)
National Museum of African Art, Smithsonian Institution, Bequest of Eliot Elisofon, 73-7-758

Cameo Parure, ca. 1820 [91]
Italy
Gold, shell, brass, leather, silk
Box: 10 x 13 x 13 inches (25.4 x 33 x 33 cm)
Peabody Essex Museum, museum purchase with funds from the Jane A. and George H Mifflin Charitable Estate, 1975, 119928

Chinese Marriage Procession and Country Views, 1816 [35]
Guangzhou, China, for the Western market
Gouache on paper
Image: 15 x 19 inches (38.1 x 48.3 cm)
Closed: 17 1/2 x 21 1/4 x 2 inches (44.5 x 54 x 2.5 cm)
Peabody Essex Museum, gift of Mr. & Mrs. John Dominis Holt, 1976, E83610.11

Door Lintel, late 18th century [67]
Karnataka, South India
Carved hardwood
11 3/4 x 44 x 2 inches (29.9 x 111.8 x 5.1 cm)
Minneapolis Institute of Arts, gift of Alfred and Ingrid Lenz Harrison, 91.14

Dowry Chest, ca. 1935 [34]
Yin Yu Tang House, Anhui Province, China
Wood, paper, paint, brass
Closed: 13 5/8 x 24 1/4 x 17 inches (34.6 x 61.6 x 43.2)
Anonymous loan

Embroidered Chest Cover, early 20th century [128]
Morocco
Cotton, silk embroidery
38 1/2 x 60 3/4 inches (97.8 x 154.3 cm)
Minneapolis Institute of Arts, gift of the Betty J. Sullivan Unitrust, 2001.3.2

Floral Mosaic, Carriage Cushion Cover, c. 1800 [28]
Sweden
Tapestry woven wool and linen
20 1/2 x 45 2/7 inches (52 x 115 cm)
The Khalili Collection of Swedish Textile Art, Inv. no. sw.84

Fukusa (wrapping cloth), late 19th century [63]
Japan
Silk and metallic thread embroidery
34 1/2 x 28 1/2 x 4 1/2 inches (87.6 x 72.4 x 11.4 cm)
Peabody Essex Museum, gift of Dr. William Sturgis Bigelow, 1921, E18120

Furoshiki (wrapping cloth), late 19th or early 20th century [62]
Okinawa, Japan
Ramie
51 1/2 x 54 1/2 inches (130.8 x 138.4 cm)
Peabody Essex Museum, gift of Charles G. Weld, 1910, E13737

Goeseok Morando (strange rock and peony painting), 19th century [44]
Korea
Eight panel screen, ink and color on paper
72 1/2 x 387 inches (184 x 983 cm)
Peabody Essex Museum, museum purchase and gift of Lea Sneider, 2001, E301718

Horses and Trees in Octagons, Bed Cover, 1830–1855 [30]
Scania, Sweden
Tapestry woven wool and linen
50 2/5 x 93 5/7 inches (128 x 238 cm)
The Khalili Collection of Swedish Textile Art, Inv. no. sw.73

Hwarot (bridal robe), late 18th century [104]
Seoul, Korea
Silk, paper, cotton, wool, metallic thread
52 x 72 1/2 x 19 inches (132.1 x 184.2 x 48.3 cm)
Peabody Essex Museum, museum purchase, 1927, E20190.F

Inubako (dog-shaped box), 18th century [64]
Japan
Papier-mâché, pigments, gesso
10 5/8 x 13 3/4 x 8 1/2 inches (27 x 34.9 x 21.6 cm)
Peabody Essex Museum, gift of Edward Sylvester Morse, 1898, E6570

Izikoti (wedding cape), early 20th century [115]
Zulu peoples, South Africa
Cloth, beads, metal buttons
38 9/16 x 36 5/8 x 1 3/16 inches (98 x 93 x 3 cm)
National Museum of African Art, Smithsonian Institution, museum purchase, 99-4-2

Kai-Awase (shell matching game), late 17th–18th century [65]
Japan
Paper, wood, pigments, and shells
Box: 14 x 13 5/8 inches (35.6 x 34.6 cm)
Peabody Essex Museum, gift of Dr. Charles Goddard Weld, 1908, E10401 and E10402

Kirogi (wedding duck), 19th century [49]
Korea
Wood with traces of ink
9 1/2 x L 13 1/2 inches (24.1 x 34.3 cm)
Brooklyn Museum, gift of Mr. and Mrs. Alastair B. Martin, the Guennol Collection, 86.140

Marriage Certificate of John and Elizabeth Blandin, ca. 1825 [75]
Pennsylvania
Paper
11 7/8 x 15 9/16 inches (30.2 x 39.5 cm)
The Metropolitan Museum of Art, Rogers Fund, 1944, 44.109.8

Marriage Contract for Marriage of Esther Borgho and Abraham Borgho, ca. 1700 **[74]**
Siena, Italy
Ink, gouache, and gold leaf on parchment
32 11/16 x 22 7/8 inches (83 x 58.3 cm)
The Jewish Museum, New York, Gift of Dr. Harry G. Friedman, F 2407

Moon Shawl, ca. 1801 **[4]**
Kashmir
Goats' fleece
64 1/2 x 65 3/4 inches (163.8 x 167 cm)
Peabody Essex Museum, gift of the Estate of Charlotte Saunders Nichols, 1938, 123590

Nuptial Crown, ca. 1884 **[10]**
St. Petersburg, Russia
Silver, diamonds, velvet
5 3/4 x 4 inches (dia.) (14.6 x 10.2 cm)
Hillwood Estate, Museum & Gardens; bequest of Marjorie Merriweather Post, 1973, 17.63

Odhani (woman's wedding headcover), late 19th–early 20th century **[109]**
Kutch, Gujarat, India
Silk satin with tie dye (bandhani) and metallic-thread embroidery
69 1/2 x 60 inches (176.5 x 152.4 cm)
Los Angeles County Museum of Art, Costume Council Fund, M.60.31

Preparations for a Court Wedding, mid-Edo period, 18th century **[37]**
Japan
Hanging scroll; color and ink on paper
Image: 12 7/8 x 35 3/4 inches (32.7 x 90.8 cm)
Los Angeles County Museum of Art, purchased with funds provided by the President's Circle Sponsors 2001 Japan Tour, M2001.142

Qmajja (wedding tunic), 19th century
Tunisia, North Africa
Silk, cotton, sequins, beads, metallic thread
52 x 45 inches (132.1 x 114.3 cm)
National Museum of African Art, Smithsonian Institution, gift in memory of Brian and Eleanor DeLiagre Aherne, Smithsonian Institution, 2001-19-2

Rain Sash and Case, 20th century **[61]**
Hopi
Sash: Cotton
49 x 10 x 98 inches (124.5 x 25.4 x 248.9 cm)
Peabody Essex Museum, gift of Mrs. Peter Seamans, 2007, E303557
Case: Reed, cotton
28 3/4 x 111 inches (73 x 282 cm)
Peabody Museum of Archaeology and Ethnology

Seed Pearl Parure, ca. 1845 **[92]**
United States
Seed pearls, mother-of-pearl, gold, silk, leather, wood, cardboard
Box: 9 3/4 x 10 1/2 x 9 inches (24.8 x 26.7 x 22.9 cm)
Peabody Essex Museum, estate of Fanny P. Mason, 1949, 127662

Spear Blade Currency, 19th century **[26]**
Lokele or Turumbu peoples, Democratic Republic of the Congo
Iron
70 x 15 5/8 inches (177.8 x 39.7 cm)
National Museum of African Art, Smithsonian Institution, museum purchase, 83-3-14

Suzani, 19th century **[27]**
Shahrisabs, Uzbekistan
Cotton, silk embroidery
76 x 92 inches (193 x 233.4 cm)
Minneapolis Institute of Arts, bequest of Miss Lily Place, 30.23.27

Tabzimt (pendant), ca. 1905 **[117]**
Kabyle peoples, Kabylie, Algeria
Silver alloy, coral, enamel
5 9/16 x 4 5/16 x 13/16 inches (14.2 x 11 x 2 cm)
National Museum of African Art, Smithsonian Institution, gift of Mr. and Mrs. James Phoenix in memory of Charlotte MacFadden, 92-11-1

Uchikake (outer robe), Edo period, 19th century **[107]**
Japan
Satin damask (rinzu) with resist dyeing and silk
66 1/2 x 45 1/2 inches (168.9 x 115.6 cm)
Museum of Fine Arts, Boston, William Sturgis Bigelow Collection, 1911, 11.3862

Uchikake (outer robe), Edo period, 19th century **[108]**
Japan
Satin damask (rinzu) with resist dyeing and silk
65 x 48 inches (165.1 x 121.9 cm)
Museum of Fine Arts, Boston, William Sturgis Bigelow Collection, 1911, 11.3833

Umlak (bridegroom's wedding crown), 19th century **[105]**
India
Repoussé silver with gilding
6 3/8 x 10 3/8 inches (16.2 x 26.4 cm)
Los Angeles County Museum of Art, Purchased with funds provided by Sunita Mula Wadhwani, Ravi Wadhwani, and Kiran Wadhwani Samuels in memory of Mulchand Navalrai Wadhwani, AC1998.54.1

Wedding Basket, early 20th century **[48]**
Diné (Navajo)
Woven plant fiber
2 1/4 x 12 1/2 inches (dia.) (5.7 x 31.8 cm)
Peabody Essex Museum, gift of Stephen Wheatland, 1951, E37259

Wedding Casket, ca. 1650 **[31]**
Friesland, Holland
Silver
4 1/4 x 3 1/2 x 2 1/2 inches (10.8 x 8.9 x 6.4 cm)
Peabody Essex Museum, gift of the American Antiquarian Society, 1941, 124287

Wedding Coat, 20th century **[113]**
Sindh, Pakistan
Silk, cotton, sequins, metallic thread, silver beads, mirrors
34 1/2 x 36 inches (87.6 x 91.4 cm)
Minneapolis Institute of Arts, gift of Richard L. Simmons, 2001.289.41

Wedding Dress, 1719 **[94]**
Cambridge, Massachusetts, made of fabric imported from England
Silk with reproduction petticoat and accessories
54 x 33 x 32 inches (137.2 x 83.8 x 81.3 cm)
Peabody Essex Museum, gift of Mrs. William W. West, 1919, 108486

Wedding Dress, 1801 **[4]**
Salem, Massachusetts, made of fabric imported from India
Cotton
50 1/2 x 22 x 21 inches (128.3 x 5.1 x 53.3 cm)
Peabody Essex Museum, gift of the Estate of Charlotte Saunders Nichols, 1938, 123571.W

Wedding Dress, 1837 **[95]**
Boston, Massachusetts
Silk, cotton, metal
51 x 32 x 24 inches (129.5 x 81.3 x 61 cm)
Peabody Essex Museum, gift of Mrs. Cornelius C. Felton, 1977, 134345.AB

Wedding Dress, ca. 1845 **[101]**
Southern United States
Cotton
39 1/2 (skirt length) 31 (chest) 25 1/2 (waist) inches (100.3 x 78.7 x 64.8 cm)
Witte Museum

Wedding Dress, 1865 **[97]**
Massachusetts
Silk, cotton, other materials
59, Bodice: 21 x 12 x 19 inches (149.9 x 53.3 x 30.5 x 48.3 cm)
Peabody Essex Museum, gift of Mrs. Delmar Leighton, 1957, 129091

Wedding Dress and Necklace, 1872 **[96]**
North Shore, Massachusetts
Dress: Silk, cotton, metal; Necklace: Stone beads
Dress: 50 x 34 x 29 inches (127 x 86.4 x 73.7 cm)
Necklace: 1/2 x 5 1/2 x 8 1/2 inches (1.3 x 14 x 21.6 cm)
Peabody Essex Museum, gift of Annie L. Cutts, 1958, 129156.1A-D, .5

Wedding Dress, 1880 **[98]**
Massachusetts
Silk, wax, cotton, metal, glass, other materials
56 x 38 x 65; train: 41 inches (142.2 x 96.5 x 165.1; 104.1 cm)
Peabody Essex Museum, gift of Ellen Poore Moseley Ames, 1980, 135025

Wedding Garments for Bride and Groom, 2004 **[112]**
Imphal, Manipur, India
Bride's wedding dress (potloi): fabric, gold, silk, cotton, seeds; 52 x 15 inches (132.1 x 38.1 cm)
Groom's cotton pumyat with buttons (kurta): fabric, cotton, seeds; 54 x 20 inches (137.2 x 50.8 cm)
Collection of The Newark Museum, purchase 2004 Willard W. Kelsey Bequest Fund, 2004.76.1; 2004.76.2

Wedding Procession, 20th century **[69]**
Yoruba culture, Nigeria
Wood, beads, cowrie shells
6 3/4 x 14 1/2 inches (17.2 x 36.8 cm)
Courtesy of Bowers Museum, Santa Ana, CA, Acquisition Fund Purchase, BMCA 77.73.1

Wedding Procession: Bride Under a Canopy, ca. 1800 **[66]**
West Bengal, Murshidabad, India
Opaque watercolor on mica
5 1/4 x 7 1/8 inches (13.3 x 18.1 cm)
Los Angeles County Museum of Art, gift of Miss Gertrude McCheyne, 37.28.9

Wedding Procession: Groom on a Horse, ca. 1800 **[68]**
West Bengal, Murshidabad, India
Opaque watercolor on mica
5 1/4 x 7 1/8 inches (13.3 x 18.1 cm)
Los Angeles County Museum of Art, gift of Miss Gertrude McCheyne, 37.28.10

Woman's Wedding Sari, 19th century **[110]**
Patan, Gujarat, India
Silk plain weave with warp- and weft-resist dye (patola) and gold metallic thread supplementary weft

176 3/4 x 46 1/2 inches (449 x 118.1 cm)
Los Angeles County Museum of Art, Costume Council Fund, M.71.37.2

Woman's Wedding Tunic and Vest, late 19th century **[103]**
China
Silk, gold metallic thread
32 11/16 x 45 2/7 inches (83 x 115 cm)
Peabody Essex Museum, gift of the Estate of Julia C. Deane, 2001, E301847

Yuinō Engagement Gifts, 2007 **[23]**
Japan
Paper cord, bamboo, balsa wood, metallic foils, glass, metal, plastic
16 1/2 x 60 x 42 inches (41.9 x 152.4 x 106.7 cm)
Peabody Essex Museum, museum purchase, 2007, E303618

FIGURE LIST

Figure 1
Vénus of Lespugue, Paleolithic period
Grotte des Rideaux à Lespugue, Haute-Garonne, France
Carved mammoth ivory
5 5/8 inches (14.7 cm)
Musée de l'Homme, Paris

Figure 2
Wendy Wahl (b. 1961)
Goddess Girdle, 1996
Rhode Island
Paper, wool, boneoid
67 x 34 inches (170.2 x 86.4 cm)
Museum of the Rhode Island School of Design, Mary B. Jackson Fund, 1998.44

Figure 3
William Hogarth (1697–1764)
Marriage à la Mode: 1. The Marriage Settlement, ca. 1743
England
Oil on canvas
35 3/4 x 27 1/2 inches (90.8 x 69.9 cm)
The National Gallery, London, NG113

Figure 4
James Ensor (1860–1949)
The Intrigue, 1911
Belgium
Oil on canvas
37 1/4 x 44 1/4 inches (34.7 x 112.4 cm); Frame 47 3/8 x 53 7/8 x 3 1/2 inches (120.3 x 136.8 x 8.9 cm)
Minneapolis Institute of Arts, The Modernism

Collection, gift of Mr. and Mrs. John S. Pillsbury, Sr., 70.38

Figure 5
Charles Webster Hawthorne (1872–1930)
The Trousseau, 1910
United States
Oil on canvas mounted on wood
40 x 40 inches (101.6 x 101.6 cm)
The Metropolitan Museum of Art, George A. Hearn Fund, 1911, 11.78

Figure 6
Bride Price, 20th century
Highlands, Papua New Guinea
Resin: tree; shell: mother of pearl; pigment: red ochre; fiber: pandanus leaf, cotton, knitted trade cloth; wood: bamboo
16 3/4 x 13 3/4 x 3/4 inches (42.5 x 34.9 x 1.9 cm)
Fine Arts Museum of San Francisco, Anonymous gift, 78.75.1

Figure 7
The Projecta Casket, ca. AD 380, Late Roman
Rome, Italy
Silver gilt
11 3/4 x 21 1/2 inches (29.9 x 54.9 cm)
The British Museum, 12-29,1

Figure 8
Theodore Robinson (1852–1896)
The Wedding March, 1892
Giverny, France
Oil on canvas
22 5/16 x 26 1/2 inches (56.7 x 67.3 cm)
Terra Foundation for American Art, Chicago, Daniel J. Terra Collection, 1999.13

Figure 9
Fra Filippo Lippi (ca. 1406–1469)
Portrait of a Woman with a Man at a Casement, ca. 1440
Florence, Italy
Tempera on wood
25 1/4 x 16 1/2 inches (64.1 x 41.9 cm)
The Metropolitan Museum of Art, Marquand Collection, Gift of Henry G. Marquand, 1889, 89.15.19

Figure 10
Frans Hals (1580–1666)
Portrait of Isaac Massa and Beatrix van der Laen, 1622
Holland
Oil on canvas
55 1/8 x 65 1/2 inches (140 x 166.5 cm)
Rijksmuseum Amsterdam, SK-A-133

Figure 11
Robert Walker (1607–ca.1659)
*Portraits of Josiah Winslow (1628–1680) and
Penelope Pelham Winslow (1630–1703)*, 1651
London
Oil on canvas
37 x 32 inches (94 x 81.3 cm)
Pilgrim Hall Museum, gift of Abby
Frothingham Gay Winslow, 1888, PHM0054
and PHM0055

Figure 12
R. B. Kitaj (1932–2007)
The Wedding, 1989-1993
England
Oil on canvas
7 1/4 x 7 1/4 inches (18.3 x 18.3 cm)
Tate, London, T06743

Figure 13
Marcel Duchamp (1887–1968)
*The Bride Stripped Bare by Her Bachelors, Even
(The Large Glass)*, 1915–1923
United States
Oil, varnish, lead foil, lead wire, and dust on
glass panels
109 1/4 x 69 inches (277.5 x 175.3 cm)
Philadelphia Museum of Art, bequest of
Katherine S. Dreier, 1952, 1952-98-1

Figure 14
Max Ernst (1891–1976)
*Attirement of the Bride (L'habillement de
l'épousée (de la mariée))*, 1940
France
Oil on canvas
51 x 38 inches (129.6 x 96.3 cm)
Solomon R. Guggenheim Foundation, Peggy
Guggenheim Collection, 1976, 76.2553 PG 78

Figure 15
Louise Nevelson (1899–1988)
Dawn's Wedding Chapel II, 1959
New York
White painted wood
115 7/8 x 83 1/2 x 10 1/2 inches (294.3 x 212.1
x 26.7 cm); Base: 6 x 83 1/2 x 10 1/2 inches
(15.2 x 212.1 x 26.7 cm)
Whitney Museum of American Art, New
York; Purchase, with funds from the Howard
and Jean Lipman Foundation, Inc., 70.68a-m

Figure 16
Kamisaka Sekka (1866–1942)
Takasago, Taishō-Shōwa period
Japan
Hanging scroll; ink and colors on silk
55 3/4 x 19 3/4 inches (141.7 x 50.4 cm)
The Clark Center for Japanese Art & Culture,
1997.13

Figure 17
Queen Victoria's Wedding Dress, 1840
England
Silk
The Royal Collection

Figure 18
*Marriage Certificate of Isaac Jones and
Sophronia Rand*, 1853
Weston, Massachusetts
Engraving on paper
14 x 11 inches (35.6 x 27.9 cm)
Courtesy, The Winterthur Library: Joseph
Downs Collection of Manuscripts and Printed
Ephemera, Col. 211, no. 93 x 13

Figure 19
Sir George Hayter (1792–1871)
*The Marriage of Queen Victoria, 10 February
1840*, 1840–1842
England
Oil on canvas
77 x 107 5/8 inches (195.6 x 273.4 cm)
The Royal Collection

Figure 20
Richard Caton Woodville (1825–1855)
The Sailor's Wedding, 1852
Paris
Oil on canvas
18 1/8 x 22 inches (46 x 55.9 cm)
The Walters Art Museum, Baltimore, 37.142

Figure 21
Odhani (woman's wedding headcover), ca. 1940
India
Silk with tie dye, badla tachnique and metallic
thread embroidery
60 x 72 inches (182.9 x 152.4 cm)
Courtesy of Donald Clay Johnson

Figure 22
Wedding Sari, ca. 1940
India
Cotton, tie dyed with gold brocade
48 x 87 inches (221 x 122 cm)
Courtesy of Donald Clay Johnson

Figure 23
Florine Stettheimer (1871–1944)
The Cathedrals of Fifth Avenue, 1931
New York
Oil on canvas
60 x 50 inches (152.4 x 127 cm)
The Metropolitan Museum of Art, gift of Ettie
Stettheimer, 1953, 53.24.4

Figure 24
Frida Kahlo (1907–1954)
*My Grandparents, My Parents, and I (Family
Tree)*, 1936
Mexico
Oil and tempera on metal panel
12 1/8 x 13 5/8 inches (30.8 x 34.6 cm)
The Museum of Modern Art, gift of Allan
Roos, M.D., and B. Mathieu Roos, 102.198

Figure 25
Gay Block (b. 1942) and Malka Drucker (b.
1945)
A Recontextualized Ketubbah, 1994
United States
Chromogenic color print
24 x 20 inches (61 x 50.8 cm)
The Jewish Museum, New York, gift of the
artists, 1994-58

Figure 26
Robert Boyd (b. 1969)
L'Age d'Or, 2001
Brooklyn, New York
Digital C-print
58 x 36 inches (147.3 x 91.4 cm)
Courtesy of the artist

PLATE 128

Embroidered Chest Cover, early 20th century / Morocco / Cotton, silk embroidery / Minneapolis Institute of Arts

SELECTED BIBLIOGRAPHY

I. American and European Weddings and Art

Arch, Nigel, and Joanna Marschner. *The Royal Wedding Dresses.* London: Sedgwick and Jackson, 1990.

Aswar, Sativa Sutan. *Antakesuma Embroidery in the Minangkabau Adat.* Jakarta: Penerbit Djambatan, 1999.

Banta, Martha. *Imaging American Women: Idea and Ideals in Cultural History.* New York: Columbia University Press, 1987.

Barndt, Deborah, ed. *Wild Fire: Art as Activism.* Toronto: Sumach Press, 2006.

Beilenson, Esther Budoff. *I Do, I Do: Traditions, Poetry, and Ideas on Courtship and Marriage.* White Plains, NY: Peter Pauper Press, 1991.

Blayney, Molly Dolan. *Wedded Bliss: A Victorian Bride's Handbook.* New York: Abbeville Press, 1992.

Bulcroft, Kris, Linda Smeins, and Richard Bulcroft. *Romancing the Honeymoon: Consummating Marriage in Modern Society.* Thousand Oaks, CA: Sage Publications, 1999.

Carter, C. F., comp. *The Wedding Day in Literature and Art: A Collection of the Best Descriptions of Weddings from the Works of the World's Leading Novelists and Poets, Richly Illustrated with Reproductions of Famous Paintings of Incidents of the Nuptial Day.* Detroit: Singing Tree Press, 1969. First published 1900 by Dodd, Mead.

Chadwick, Whitney. *Women, Art, and Society.* London: Thames & Hudson, 2002.

Cott, Nancy F. *Public Vows: A History of Marriage and the Nation.* Cambridge, MA: Harvard University Press, 2002.

Cross, Wilbur, and Ann Novotny. *White House Weddings.* New York: David McKay, 1967.

Driskell, David C. *Two Centuries of Black American Art.* Los Angeles: Los Angeles County Museum of Art in association with Alfred A. Knopf, 1976.

Emanuel, David, and Elizabeth Emanuel. *A Dress for Diana.* New York: Collins Design, 2006.

Frank, Robin Jaffee. *Love and Loss: American Portrait and Mourning Miniatures.* New Haven, CT: Yale University Art Gallery, 2000.

Freeman, Elizabeth. *The Wedding Complex: Forms of Belonging in Modern American Culture.* Durham, NC: Duke University Press, 2002.

Geller, Jaclyn. *Here Comes the Bride: Women, Weddings, and the Marriage Mystique.* New York: Four Walls Eight Windows, 2001.

Gillingham, Arnie R. "Modern Mexican Painting" (lecture at University of Pittsburgh, 1996).

Gillis, John R. *For Better, For Worse: British Marriages, 1600 to the Present.* New York: Oxford University Press, 1985.

Glass, Catherine, ed. *Speaking of Marriage.* Berkeley: Ten Speed Press, 1992.

Gruber, J. Richard, and David Houston. *The Art of the South, 1890–2003.* New Orleans: Ogden Museum of Southern Art, University of New Orleans, and Goldring-Woldenberg Institute for the Advancement of Southern Art and Culture in association with Scala Publishers, 2004.

Hall, Trevor. *A Day to Remember: The Wedding of the Prince and Princess of Wales.* New York: Crescent Books, 1982.

Haskell, Barbara. *The American Century: Art & Culture, 1900–1950.* New York: Whitney Museum of American Art in association with W.W. Norton, 1999.

Haugland, H. Kristina. *Grace Kelly: Icon of Style to Royal Bride.* Philadelphia: Philadelphia Museum of Art in association with Yale University Press, 2006.

Hook, Philip, and Mark Polimore. *Popular 19th-Century Painting: A Dictionary of European Genre Painters.* Woodbridge, Suffolk: Antique Collectors' Club, 1986.

Howard, Vicki. *Brides, Inc.: American Weddings and the Business of Tradition.* Philadelphia: University of Pennsylvania Press, 2006.

Ingraham, Chrys. *White Weddings: Romancing Heterosexuality in Popular Culture,* 2nd ed. New York: Routledge, 2008.

Jabour, Anya. *Marriage in the Early Republic: Elizabeth and William Wirt and the Companionate Ideal.* Baltimore: Johns Hopkins University Press, 1998.

Johns, Elizabeth. *American Genre Painting: The Politics of Everyday Life.* New Haven, CT: Yale University Press, 1991.

Kaplan, Marion A., ed. *The Marriage Bargain: Women and Dowries in European History.* New York: Institute for Research in History and Haworth Press,1985.

Keen, Michael. *Jewish Ritual Art in the Victoria & Albert Museum.* London: Victoria & Albert Museum and HMSO, 1991.

Lacy, Peter. *The Wedding.* New York: Grosset & Dunlap, 1969.

Lasansky, Janet. *A Good Start: The Aussteir or Dowry.* Lewisbury, PA: Oral Traditions Project, 1990.

Leeds-Hurwtiz, Wendy. *Wedding as Text: Communicating Cultural Identities Through Ritual.* Mahway, NJ: Lawrence Erlbaum, 2002.

Lipsett, Linda Otto. *To Love & To Cherish: Brides Remembered.* San Francisco: Quilt Digest Press, 1989.

Loring, John. *Magnificent Tiffany Silver.* New York: Harry N. Abrams, 2001.

———. *Paulding Farnham: Tiffany's Lost Genius.* New York: Harry N. Abrams, 2000.

———. *Tiffany Jewels.* New York: Harry N. Abrams, 1999.

———. *Tiffany's 150 Years.* Garden City, NY: Doubleday, 1987.

Manley, Roger, and Mark Sloan. *Self-Made Worlds: Visionary Folk Art Environments.* New York: Aperture Foundation, 1997.

McBride-Mellinger, Maria. *The Wedding Dress.* London: Little, Brown, 1993.

Mead, Rebecca. *One Perfect Day: The Selling of the American Wedding.* New York: Penguin Press, 2007.

Mitchell, Stephen, and Robert Hass, eds. *Into the Garden, A Wedding Anthology: Poetry and Prose on Love and Marriage.* New York: HarperCollins, 1993.

Mo, Charles L. *To Have and to Hold: 135 Years of Wedding Fashions.* Charlotte, NC: Mint Museum of Art, 2000.

Murphy, Brian. *The World of Weddings: An Illustrated Celebration.* New York: Paddington Press, 1978.

Norfleet, Barbara P. *Wedding.* Cambridge, MA: Carpenter Center for the Visual Arts, Harvard University, 1976.

Otnes, Cele C., and Elizabeth H. Pleck. *Cinderella Dreams: The Allure of the Lavish Wedding.* Berkeley: University of California Press, 2003.

Parkinson, Judy. *Edward and Sophie: A Royal Wedding.* Chicago: Contemporary Books, 1999.

Perry, Regina A. *Free Within Ourselves: African-American Artists in the Collection of the National Museum of American Art.* Washington, DC: National Museum of American Art, Smithsonian Institution, in association with Pomegranate Artbooks, 1992.

Probert, Christina. *Brides in Vogue Since 1910.* New York: Abbeville Press, 1984.

Quine, Judith Balaban. *The Bridesmaids: Grace Kelly, Princess of Monaco, and Six Intimate Friends.* New York: Weidenfeld & Nicolson, 1989.

Roderick, Kyle. *Married in the Movies.* San Francisco: Collins Publishers San Francisco, 1994.

Roney, Carley. *The Knot: The Ultimate Wedding Planner.* New York: Broadway Books, 1999.

Rothman, Ellen K. *Hands and Hearts: A History of Courtship in America.* Cambridge, MA: Harvard University Press, 1987.

Schreier, Sandy. *Hollywood Gets Married.* New York: Clarkson Potter, 2002.

Scoble, Gretchen, and Ann Field. *The Meaning of Wedding Anniversaries.* San Francisco: Chronicle Books, 2004.

Seligson, Marcia. *The Eternal Bliss Machine: American Way of Wedding.* New York: William Morrow, 1973.

Smith, Marie, and Louise Durbin. *White House Brides: A New and Revealing History of Romance and Courtship in the President's Mansion.* Washington, DC: Acropolis Books, 1966.

Stewart, Martha. *Weddings.* New York: Clarkson Potter, 1987.

Tober, Barbara. *The Bride: A Celebration.* Stamford, CT: Longmeadow Press for Condé Nast Publications, 1984.

Trechsel, Gail Andrews. *Pictured in My Mind: Contemporary American Self-Taught Art from the Collection of Dr. Kurt Gitter and Alice Rae Yelen.* Birmingham, AL: Birmingham Museum of Art, 1996.

Waggoner, Susan. *I Do! I Do!: From the Veil to the Vows—How Classic Wedding Traditions Came to Be.* New York: Rizzoli, 2002.

Wallace, Carol McD. *All Dressed in White: The Irresistible Rise of the American Wedding.* New York: Penguin Books, 2004.

Wang, Vera. *Vera Wang on Weddings.* New York: HarperResource, 2001.

Wood, Christopher. *Victorian Painters*. Woodbridge, Suffolk: Antique Collectors' Club, 1995.

II. International Weddings and Art

Baldizzone, Tiziana, and Gianni Baldizzone. *Wedding Ceremonies, Ethnic Symbols, Costume and Rituals*. Paris: Flammarion, 2001.

———. *Hidden Tribes of India*. London: Local Colours, 2000.

———. *Brahmaputra, Tales from the River: Tibet, India, Bangladesh*. Boston: Shambhala, 1998.

———. *Tibet, Journey to the Forbidden City: In the Footsteps of Alexandra David-Neel*. New York: Stewart,Tabori and Chang, 1997.

Basham, A.L. *The Wonder That Was India*. Delhi: Rupa, 1998.

Ben-Ari, Eyal, Brian Moeran, and James Valentine. *Unwrapping Japan: Society and Culture in Anthropological Perspective*. Honolulu: University of Hawaii Press, 1990.

Bernus, E. *Touaregs Nigeriens*. Paris: ORSTOM, 1981.

Bhandari, V., and R. Kashyap. *Celebrating Dreams: Weddings in India*. Delhi: Prakash Books, 1999.

Corrigan, Gina. *Miao Textiles from China*. Seattle: University of Washington Press, 2001.

Dabing, Ye, comp. *The Bride's Boat: Marriage Customs of China's Fifty-five Ethnic Minorities*. Beijing: New World Press, 1993.

Dupire, M. *Organisation Sociale des Peuls*. Paris: Plon, 1970.

———. *Peuls Nomades*. Paris: Institute d'Ethnologie, 1962.

Edwards, Walter. *Modern Japan Through Its Weddings: Gender, Person, and Society in Ritual Portrayal*. Stanford, CA: Stanford University Press, 1989.

Fabled Cloths of Minangkabau. Santa Barbara, CA: Santa Barbara Museum of Art, 1997.

Frey, Katherine Stenger. *Journey to the Land of the Earth Goddess*. Jakarta: Gramedia Publishing, 1986.

Foster, Helen Bradley, and Donald Clay Johnson, eds. *Wedding Dress Across Cultures*. New York: Berg, 2003.

Gabriel, Hannalore. *The Jewelry of Nepal: Splendor in Symbols*. New York: Weatherhill, 1999.

Gittinger, Mattibelle. *Textiles and the Tai Experience in Southeast Asia*. Washington, DC: Textile Museum, 1992.

Grossman, Grace Cohen, ed. *Romance & Ritual: Celebrating the Jewish Wedding*. Los Angeles: Skirball Cultural Center in association with the University of Washington Press, 2001.

Guanya, Zhu. *Clothing and Ornaments of China's Miao People*. Trans. Wang Rongda. Beijing: Cultural Palace of Nationalities, 1985.

Hendry, Joy. *Marriage in Changing Japan: Community and Society*. New York: St. Martin's Press, 1981.

Kapchan, Deborah. *Gender on the Market: Moroccan Women and the Revoicing of Tradition*. Philadelphia: University of Pennsylvania Press, 1996.

Kendall, Laurel. *Getting Married in Korea: Of Gender, Morality, and Modernity*. Berkeley: University of California Press, 1996.

Krishna, Nanditha. *Arts and Crafts of Tamilnadu*. Middletown, NJ: Grantha, 1992.

Kuper, Adam. *Wives for Cattle: Bridalwealth and Marriage in Southern Africa*. London: Routledge, 1982.

Laoust, Emile, *Noces Berbère: Les cérémonies du Mariage au Maroc*. Aix-en-Provence: Edisud; Paris: La Boite à Documents, 1993.

Life Styles of China's Ethnic Minorities. Hong Kong: Peace Book Co., 1991.

Mack, J. *Ethnic Jewellery*. London: British Museum Publications, 1988.

Mackie, Louise W. *The Threads of Time in Fez, Morocco*. (Article from website of the Royal Ontario Museum)

Mariages d'Ailleurs. (Various authors). Paris: Musée de l'Homme, 1995.

Mordecai, Carolyn. *Weddings: Dating and Love Customs of Cultures Worldwide, Including Royalty*. Phoenix, AZ: Nittany Publishers, 1999.

Murphy, Veronica, and Rosemary Crill. *Tie-dyed Textiles of India: Tradition and Trade*. New York: Rizzoli, 1991.

Murra, John V. "Cloth and Its Function in the Inca State," in *Cloth and Human Experience,* ed. J. Weiner and J. Schneider. Washington, DC: Smithsonian Institution Press, 1989.

Nabokov, Isabelle. *Religion Against the Self: An Ethnography of Tamil Rituals*. Oxford: Oxford University Press, 2000.

Nicolaisen, Johannes. *The Pastoral Tuareg: Ecology, Culture and Society*. New York: Thames & Hudson, 1997.

Pandey, Rajbali. *Hindu Samskaras*. New Delhi: Motilal Banarsidas, 1998.

Pandolfi, P. *Les Touaregs de l'Ahaggar*. Paris: Karthala, 1998.

Rabatè, J., and M. R. Rabatè. *Bijoux du Maroc*. Aix-en-Provence: Edisud/Le Fennec, 1996.

Rabatè, M. R., and A. Goldenberg. *Bijoux du Maroc*. Aix-en-Provence: Edisud, 1999.

Stack, Lotus. "A Wedding at Fez: Textiles in Transition." *Saudi Aramco World* (May/June 1993).

Summerfield, Anne, and John Summerfield, eds. *Walk in Splendor: Ceremonial Dress and the Minangkabau*. Los Angeles: UCLA Fowler Museum of Cultural History, 1999.

Spencer, A. *Les Lapons, Peuple du Renne*. Paris: Armand Colin, 1985.

Tarlo, Emma. *Clothing Matters: Dress and Its Symbolism in Modern India*. Chicago: University of Chicago Press, 1996.

Thomas, P. *Hindu Religion Customs and Manners*. Bombay: Taraporevala Sons, 1969.

Tufte, Virginia. *High Wedlock Then Be Honored: Wedding Poems from Nineteen Countries and Twenty-five Centuries*. New York: Viking Press, 1970.

Van Offelen, M., and C. Beckwith. *Nomads of Niger*. London: Collins, 1984.

Westermarck, Edward. *Marriage Ceremonies in Morocco*. 2nd ed. London: Curzon Press; Totowa, NJ, Rowman & Littlefield, 1972.

———. *Les Cérémonies du Mariages au Maroc*. Paris: Editions Leroux, 1921.

Yin, Ma, ed. *China's Minority Nationalities*. Beijing: Foreign Languages Press, 1989.

Ziran, Bai. *Moeurs et Coutumes des Miao*. Beijing: Editions en Langues Etrangères, 1988.

III. Historical Sources

An Accurate Description of the Marriage Ceremonies Used by Every Nation in the World. Shewing the Oddity of Some, the Absurdity of Others, the Drollery of Many; and the Real or Intended Piety of All. Boston: Printed by Joseph White, 1802.

Alcott, William A. *The Physiology of Marriage.* Boston: John P. Jewett, 1859.

———. *The Young Husband.* Boston: George W. Light, 1839.

———. *The Young Wife, or Duties of Woman in the Marriage Relationship.* Boston: George W. Light, 1837.

The American Spectator, or Matrimonial Preceptor. A Collection of Essays, Epistles, Precepts, and Examples, Relating to the Married State, From the Most Celebrated Writers, Ancient and Modern, Adapted to the State of Society in the American Republic. Boston: Manning & Loring, 1797.

The Bazar Book of the Household. New York: Harper & Brothers, 1875.

Carroll, George D. *Wedding Etiquette and Usages of Polite Society.* New York: Dempsey & Carroll, 1880.

Case, Carleton. *The American Girl in Society: The Way to Social Success, Showers for the Bride, Wedding Etiquette.* Chicago: Shrewsbury, 1916.

Chatelain, Clara de. *Bridal Etiquette: A Sensible Guide to the Etiquette and Observances of the Marriage Ceremonies.* New York: Dick & Fitzgerald, n.d. [ca. 1870].

Clark, Jean Wilde. *A Desk Book on the Etiquette of Social Stationery.* New York: Eaton, Cranke and Pike, 1910.

Fowler, L. N. *Marriage, Its History and Ceremonies, with a Phrenological and Physiological Exposition of the Functions and Qualifications for Happy Marriages.* New York: Fowlers and Wells, Phrenological Cabinet, 1848.

Good Form Weddings Formal and Informal. New York: Frederick A. Stokes, 1891.

Kingsland, Mrs. Burton. *The Book of Weddings: A Complete Manual of Good Form in All Matters Connected with the Marriage Ceremony.* New York: Doubleday, 1902.

Learned, Mrs. Frank. *The Etiquette of New York Today.* New York: Frederick A. Stokes, 1906.

Marriage Costumes of Various Nations. London: R. Ackermann, n.d.

Martine, Arthur. *How to Woo and How to Win: Containing Rules for the Etiquette of Courtship; with Directions Showing How to Begin and End a Courtship; and How Love Letters Should be Written.* New York: Dick & Fitzgerald Publishers, n.d. [ca. 1870].

The Party Table and Its Favors. Dennison Manufacturing, 1922.

Peale, Charles W. *An Essay to Promote Domestic Happiness.* Philadelphia: n.p., 1812

Phillips, S. *The Christian Home, as It Is in the Sphere of Nature and the Church.* Springfield, MA: Gurdon Bill, 1868.

A Present for an Apprentice: or, a Sure Guide to Gain Both Esteem and Estate. Philadelphia: J. Crukshank, for James Williamson, in Wilmington, 1774.

Rondout, Professor. *The Bliss of Marriage: The Way to the Altar. Matrimony Made Easy, or How to Win a Lover.* New York: Published by the author, 1854.

Secrets of Success in Love, Courtship and Marriage, Showing Also How to Obtain and Retain Health and Wealth. Newark, NJ: Union Publishing, 1879/1881.

Sherwood, Mrs. John. *Manners and Social Usages.* New York: Harper & Brothers, 1897.

Weddings and Wedding Anniversaries. London: Butterick, 1899.

Wood, Edward J. *The Wedding Day in All Ages and Countries.* New York: Harper Brothers, 1869.

CREDITS

p. 1: plate 1 Photograph © 2008 Museum of Fine Arts, Boston

p. 5: plate 3 Art © Alex Katz/ Licensed by VAGA, New York, NY

pp. 12–13: plate 4 Photograph by Dennis Helmar

p. 15: plate 5 © American Antiquarian Society

p. 16: plate 6 Photograph by Dennis Helmar

p. 21: plate 10 Photograph by Edward Owen

p. 23: plate 12 Photograph by Dennis Helmar

p. 24: plate 13 (detail) Image © The Metropolitan Museum of Art

p. 26: fig. 2 Wendy Wahl, Photograph by Erik Gould

p. 27: fig. 3 Photo © The National Gallery, London

p. 28: plate 14 © The Colonial Williamsburg Foundation; plate 15 © The Colonial Williamsburg Foundation

p. 29: plate 16 © The Colonial Williamsburg Foundation; plate 17 © The Colonial Williamsburg Foundation

p. 33: plate 20 Image © The Metropolitan Museum of Art

p. 35: plate 23 Photograph by Dennis Helmar

p. 36: plate 24 Photograph by Dennis Helmar; plate 25 Photograph by Dennis Helmar

p. 37: fig. 4 © 2008 Artists Rights Society (ARS), New York; fig. 5 Image © The Metropolitan Museum of Art

p. 38: plate 26 Photograph by Franko Khoury; fig. 6 Photograph by Joseph McDonald

p. 42: plate 31 Photograph by Dennis Helmar; fig. 7 © The Trustees of the British Museum

p. 43: plate 32 Photograph by Dennis Helmar

p. 45: plate 34 Photograph by Mark Sexton

pp. 46–47: plate 35 Photograph by Jeffrey R. Dykes

p. 48: plate 36 Photograph by Mark Sexton; fig. 8 © Terra Foundation for American Art, Chicago/Art Resource, NY

p. 49: plate 37 Photograph © 2007 Museum Associates/LACMA

p. 50: fig. 9 © The Metropolitan Museum of Art

p. 53: plate 39 © 2007 Estate of Pablo Picasso / Artists Rights Society (ARS), New York, Image © The Metropolitan Museum of Art; plate 40 Image © The Metropolitan Museum of Art

p. 54: fig. 12 © R.B. Kitaj, courtesy of Marlborough Fine Art, Image Tate, London 2007

p. 56: plate 42 Photograph by Jeffrey R. Dykes and Mark Sexton

p. 57: fig. 13 © Artists Rights Society (ARS) New York ADAGP, Paris Estate of Marcel Duchamp, Photograph by Graydon Wood; fig. 14 © 2008 Artists Rights Society (ARS), New York ADAGP, Paris

p. 59: plate 43 Photograph by Walter Silver and Dennis Helmar

p. 61: plate 44 Photograph by Mark Sexton

p. 63: fig. 15 © 2008 Estate of Louise Nevelson Artists Rights Society (ARS), New York, Photograph by Jerry L. Thompson, N.Y.

p. 64: plate 48 Photograph by Dennis Helmar

p. 65: plate 50 Photograph by Dennis Helmar; plate 51 Photograph by Franko Khoury

p. 66: plate 52 © The Colonial Williamsburg Foundation

p. 67: plate 53 © 2007 Tiffany & Co. Archives; plate 55 © 2007 Tiffany & Co. Archives

p. 68: plate 56 © 2007 Tiffany & Co. Archives

p. 69: plate 58 © 2007 Tiffany & Co. Archives; plate 60 Image © The Metropolitan Museum of Art

p. 72: plate 61 Photograph by Dennis Helmar

p. 74: plate 62 Photograph by Walter Silver; plate 63 Photograph by Walter Silver

p. 75: plate 64 Photograph by Dennis Helmar; plate 65 Photograph by Dennis Helmar

p. 76: plate 66 Photograph © 2007 Museum Associates/LACMA

p. 77: plate 68 Photograph © 2007 Museum Associates/LACMA; plate 69 Photograph by Don Wiechec

pp. 78–79: plate 70 © 2007 The Jacob and Gwendolyn Lawrence Foundation, Seattle / Artists Rights Society (ARS), New York, Photograph by Robert Lifson

p. 80: plate 72 Photograph © 2008 Museum of Fine Arts, Boston; plate 73 Photograph © 2008 Museum of Fine Arts, Boston

p. 81: plate 74 Photograph by Ardon Bar-Hama © The Jewish Museum, New York Art Resource, NY; plate 75 Image © The Metropolitan Museum of Art

p. 82: plate 76 Photograph by Jeffrey R. Dykes and Mark Sexton

pp. 83–84: plate 78 Image © Board of Trustees, National Gallery of Art, Washington

p. 86: plate 79 © Tiziana and Gianni Baldizzone

p. 91: plate 80 © Tiziana and Gianni Baldizzone

p. 95: plate 81 © Tiziana and Gianni Baldizzone

pp. 98–99: plate 82 © Tiziana and Gianni Baldizzone

pp. 102–103: plate 83 © Tiziana and Gianni Baldizzone

pp. 106–107: plate 84 © Tiziana and Gianni Baldizzone

p. 108: plate 85 © Tiziana and Gianni Baldizzone

p. 111: plate 86 © Tiziana and Gianni Baldizzone

p. 114: plate 87 © 2007 Artists Rights Society (ARS), New York / ADAGP, Paris, Image © The Metropolitan Museum of Art

p. 116: plate 88 Photograph by Jeffrey R. Dykes

pp. 116–117 plate 89 Photograph by Joe Budd

p. 117: plate 90 Photograph by Jeffrey R. Dykes

p. 118: fig. 17 The Royal Collection © 2007 Her Majesty Queen Elizabeth II, Image Museum of London

p. 119: fig. 19 The Royal Collection © 2007 Her Majesty Queen Elizabeth II

p. 121: fig. 20 © The Walters Art Museum

p. 122: plate 91 Photograph by Jeffrey R. Dykes

p. 123: plate 92 Photograph by Dennis Helmar

p. 124: plate 93 Photograph by Walter Silver

p. 125: plate 94 Photograph by Walter Silver

pp. 126–127: plate 95 Photograph on page 126 by Dennis Helmar; Photograph on page 127 by Walter Silver

pp. 128–129: plate 96 Photograph on p. 128 by Dennis Helmar; Photograph on p. 129 by Walter Silver

pp. 130–131: plate 97 Photograph on p. 130 by Walter Silver; Detail photograph on p. 131 by Dennis Helmar

pp. 132–133: plate 98 Photograph on p. 132 by Walter Silver; Photograph on p. 133 by Dennis Helmar

pp. 134–135: plate 99 Photograph on p. 134 by Walter Silver; Detail photographs on p. 135 by Dennis Helmar

pp. 136–137: plate 100 Photographs by Dennis Helmar

p. 139: plate 102 Photograph courtesy of the Indianapolis Museum of Art Photography Department

p. 140: plate 103 Photograph by Dennis Helmar

pp. 142–143: plate 104 Photograph by Dennis Helmar

p. 144: plate 105 Photograph © 2007 Museum Associates/LACMA

p. 145: plate 106 Photograph by Dennis Helmar

p. 146: plate 107 Photograph © 2008 Museum of Fine Arts, Boston

p. 147: plate 108 Photograph © 2008 Museum of Fine Arts, Boston

p. 149: plate 109 Photograph © 2007 Museum Associates/LACMA; fig. 21 Photograph by Walter Silver

PLATE 129

Bridal Headdress, 19th century / China / Kingfisher feathers, silk, enamel, brass, beads, pearls, semiprecious stones / Peabody Essex Museum

INDEX

Numbers in *italics* refer to pages with pictures.